"With record rates of stress and mental health issues in adolescents right now, this is the right book at the right time for the people who need it most."

> —**Christopher Willard, PsyD**, coauthor of
> *The Breathing Book*, and faculty at Harvard
> Medical School

"Few things are harder than being a teenager these days, and perhaps the only thing more difficult (for those of us who are not) is how to speak in an engaging and meaningful way *to* teenagers. Karen Bluth does a remarkable job of sharing this crucial practice of self-compassion in language and through examples that are interesting, relatable, and compelling. This is a book that teens (and their parents) will find practical and powerful, and I have no doubt that it will ease a lot of suffering."

> —**Steven D. Hickman, PsyD**, clinical psychologist,
> and executive director of the Center for Mindful
> Self-Compassion

"During these stressful times, teens in particular may feel caught up in confusion, uncertainty, and stress. It's all too easy to become overwhelmed by self-criticism and social comparison. *The Self-Compassionate Teen* lets you take control of your life, while building happiness, emotional strength, and more ease in your social world."

—**Mark Bertin, MD**, developmental pediatrician, and author of *How Children Thrive* and *Mindful Parenting for ADHD*

"Chock-full of useful information, potent case studies, and hands-on exercises and links, this book will be an invaluable resource for schools, parents, and anyone interested in learning how to approach life with deep compassion and care. It is especially ideal for people helping youth learn to healthfully navigate negative self-talk and feelings arising from negative self-comparison, difficult relationships, feeling different, or simply being an adolescent."

—**Janis Whitlock, PhD, MPH**, research scientist at Cornell University, founder and director of the Self-Injury and Recovery Resources research program at Cornell University, and coauthor of *Healing Self-Injury*

"Karen Bluth is one of the world's leading experts on self-compassion for teens. This well-written book shows teens how to be kind to themselves in the midst of daily challenges such as school, body image, and social media. After switching from self-criticism to self-compassion for just one moment, you'll probably be convinced. You might be giving yourself the biggest favor of your life."

—**Christopher Germer, PhD**, faculty at Harvard Medical School, and cocreator of the Mindful Self-Compassion program

"Most teens—and most humans—struggle with fear, insecurity, self-doubt, anxiety, and depression for time to time; and some of us suffer with these experiences day in and day out. Regardless of whether you experience these feelings rarely or often, this book offers simple, practical skills for treating yourself with the kindness and support you would offer a good friend, which is to say the kindness and support you absolutely deserve. So, before your unkind mind starts with its 'yes, buts' and starts telling you its usual lies about what a loser you are, open this book and begin. By reading this book and doing the practices, you will remember that you are lovable *exactly as you are*."

—**Amy Saltzman, MD**, author of *A Still Quiet Place for Teens*

"*The Self-Compassionate Teen* is more than just a book. It's the voice of your best friend, who sees who you truly are—loving, wise, strong, and brave. Soon, you discover that this best friend has been a part of you all along. Soon, you learn how to be your own best friend, especially in those hard moments when you need a best friend the most. You can do it, and this book can show you the way."

—**Dzung X. Vo, MD**, author of *The Mindful Teen*

the self-compassionate teen

mindfulness & compassion skills to conquer your critical inner voice

KAREN BLUTH, PhD

Instant Help Books
An Imprint of New Harbinger Publications, Inc.

Publisher's Note

Distributed in Canada by Raincoast Books

Copyright © 2020 by Karen Bluth
        Instant Help Books
        An imprint of New Harbinger Publications, Inc.
        5674 Shattuck Avenue
        Oakland, CA 94609
        www.newharbinger.com

Cover design by Amy Shoup

Acquired by Tesilya Hanauer

Edited by Teja Watson

Library of Congress Cataloging-in-Publication Data

Names: Bluth, Karen, author. | Neff, Kristin, author.
Title: The self-compassionate teen : mindfulness and self-compassion skills to help you conquer
    your critical inner voice / Karen Bluth, Kristin Neff.
Description: Oakland, CA : New Harbinger Publications, [2020] | Includes bibliographical
    references.
Identifiers: LCCN 2020015695 (print) | LCCN 2020015696 (ebook) | ISBN 9781684035274 (trade
    paperback) | ISBN 9781684035281 (pdf) | ISBN 9781684035298 (epub)
Subjects: LCSH: Self-esteem in adolescence--Juvenile literature. | Self-acceptance--Juvenile
    literature. | Compassion--Juvenile literature. | Mindfulness (Psychology)--Juvenile literature.
Classification: LCC BF724.3.S36 B58 2020 (print) | LCC BF724.3.S36 (ebook) | DDC 155.5/191--dc23
LC record available at https://lccn.loc.gov/2020015695
LC ebook record available at https://lccn.loc.gov/2020015696

Printed in the United States of America

22   21   20

10 9 8 7 6 5 4 3 2 1   First Printing

This book is dedicated to all teens everywhere.
May your journey through the teen years be
a little easier because of this book.

Contents

Acknowledgments

I am profoundly grateful for many who have helped bring this book to fruition. First, this book and so much of my work is built on the work of Chris Germer and Kristin Neff. Their Mindful Self-Compassion program for adults is the foundation for much of my work creating curricula for teens, including this book—many of the exercises in this book have their origin in the Mindful Self-Compassion program. I would also like to thank Lorraine Hobbs, my co-developer of Making Friends with Yourself: A Mindful Self-Compassion Program for Teens; some of the exercises in this book come from that program. Steve Hickman, director of the Center for Mindful Self-Compassion, has also provided untold stewardship and guidance in steering the teen self-compassion ship. I have tremendous respect for his wisdom, unending patience, and his creative ability to think of out-of-the-box solutions.

Laura Prochnow Phillips—my self-compassion co-teacher extraordinaire, with whom I've taught more than forty self-compassion classes—read multiple drafts of this book. Because Laura knows the nuances of practicing and teaching self-compassion, and has a great deal of experience teaching teens, her feedback has been invaluable. Syd West, a teenager who has taken our Making Friends with Yourself class, also read through early drafts of chapters and provided much-needed feedback from the perspective of a teen, as did another teen, Ned Kubica. Sanjana Shashikant Rao, a university student well-versed in self-compassion research, provided feedback on early drafts as well. Mackenzie Gill, my twenty-seven-year-old daughter, read through chapters and provided input that could only come from a daughter, such as "Mom, don't say that! You sound like a boomer!" Finally, Russell Toomey, an expert on LGBTQIA+ teen research and programs who also has experience with compassion interventions, provided important feedback on chapter 9.

I would also like to thank my editor Tesilya Hanauer at New Harbinger. Tesilya is more than an editor to me—she's become a friend I trust, whose opinion matters to me, that I really enjoy spending time with. I've learned that, when writing a book, it's so important to have people who understand you and what you're trying to get across, in addition to knowing the craft of writing; these people can tell you not only what's going well with your writing, but more importantly, tell you what isn't going well, so that you can improve the book. Tesilya does this beautifully. I also appreciate the feedback from my editor Caleb Beckwith. Caleb always responded quickly to my questions in emails, provided specific suggestions on how to move forward with my writing, and helped me navigate the challenges and logistics involved with producing this kind of book.

Most of all, I owe any success I have to my beloved partner, Dale, for his constant support while I pursue my passion for making the journey through adolescence a bit easier for teens. Dale has spent endless hours waiting for me to finish a chapter, send "just one more email," and look up from my computer so that he can ask me what I would like him to prepare for dinner.

For all of those whose effort and talents have contributed to this book, I thank you with a full heart.

Foreword

Being a teen in today's world isn't so easy. There's so much stress and pressure: school, post-graduation plans, peer groups, friends, parents, dating, and wondering where you fit into it all. You might also be experiencing conflicts with your parents as you try to forge your own way in the world. Living with all this stress takes its toll, and many teens don't know how to deal with all the pain and tension. So they may end up struggling with anxiety and depression, or use unhealthy ways of coping such as eating disorders, substance abuse, or self-injury.

Life as an adolescent has always been challenging, but it is becoming even more difficult. There is the constant stimulation of social media, worries over climate change and school shootings, and even the political state of our country and world. These external factors sit against a backdrop of internal factors such as rapid growth of the brain and body, changes in relationships with parents, and becoming a sexual being. In the midst of all this chaos, it can feel like not much is constant, that there is nothing stable to count on.

While we can't control what is happening to us, we can choose how to respond to ourselves in the midst of our struggles. We can choose to be warm and kind to ourselves rather than cold and critical. Self-compassion provides a stable source of support to help us deal with the imperfection of life, and to accept our own human imperfection. Compassion comes from the Latin *pati*, meaning to suffer (think passion), and *com*, meaning with/together. When we struggle, we can turn toward our own pain with feelings of care and connection, remembering that everyone struggles in their own way. Regardless of what is happening, self-compassion allows you to be a reliable and loving friend toward yourself—a presence that can support and encourage you as you deal with whatever comes your way. Even on rotten days when it feels like your whole world is falling apart and you can't do anything right, you can still rely on self-compassion, knowing that you have a devoted friend within you. What a relief it is to know that you always have someone you can count on!

I have devoted my life to researching the benefits of self-compassion. We know from more than 2500 research studies that self-compassion is good for you. People who are more self-compassionate experience less stress, anxiety, and depression; are happier and more satisfied with their lives; and are stronger and more resilient in the face of challenges. They are also more giving to others in relationships, more motivated, more responsible, physically healthier, and take better care of themselves. Research shows that self-compassion benefits teens just as much as adults.

In this book, Dr. Karen Bluth offers you self-compassion tools to integrate into your daily life. You can use self-compassion when you are feeling alone, while on social media, when you encounter academic stress or peer pressure, or as you negotiate your sexual or gender identity. Dr. Bluth is one of the creators of the teen version of the adult Mindful Self-Compassion program that I developed with Dr. Chris Germer. Some of the practices and exercises included in this book Dr. Bluth adapted from the adult program, and others are borrowed from the teen program, which is called *Making Friends with Yourself*. Other practices are brand new. The practices are fun, easy to do, and require no advanced knowledge or experience.

The great thing about many of the practices included in this book is that they can be implemented on the go, wherever you are, in the moment you are struggling. Longer guided meditations are also included if you want to deepen and strengthen your self-compassion practice. These longer, formal guided meditations can be practiced by setting aside a few minutes each day. It's helpful as well that downloadable recordings can be accessed via the New Harbinger website—you can play these recordings while you are engaging in the practices or exercises.

I wish I had known about self-compassion when I was a teen. If you start the habit of being a good friend to yourself now, you'll have this resource to draw upon for a lifetime. It's something you can rely upon whenever you're hurting—psychologically, emotionally, or physically. So, it's time to get started… You've got the toolbox in your hands. All you have to do is turn the page!

—Kristin Neff
Co-creator of the *Mindful Self-Compassion* program and co-author of the *Mindful Self-Compassion Workbook*

Step Aside Inner Critic— Hello, Self-Compassion!

Let me take a guess. You're feeling like you're not quite enough—not smart enough, not tough enough, not pretty enough, not "man" enough. You're feeling like everyone else is way cooler than you. And no matter how hard you try, you feel—well, just a little bit…*awkward*. Uncomfortable. And it feels like everyone can see it.

You might get a reprieve from that incessant voice now and then, but then there it is again…that critical voice that doesn't leave you alone. Always there, nagging, jabbering in your ear, telling you you're not good enough, you can do better—and that every flaw you have is glaring out at the universe like a giant light bulb.

Step right up and welcome to the world of being human. Let me assure you, you are not alone. We all have that voice inside us—*especially* teens. It's in the teen years that you develop what we call "metacognition," which means that you can think about thinking. And that means that you can think about what other people think about you—like your friends. What your friends think really matters, because from an evolutionary perspective, you need to find a peer group where you belong, where you will eventually find a mate and continue the species. This basic drive to belong is buried deep within our biology, and so anything that threatens our belonging can be experienced as super dangerous.

Here's the first secret that I'll share with you: That voice? It's not the voice of truth, even though it pretends to be. Not even close. It's the voice of the inner critic, and it's there for a reason, sometimes even a good reason—but the reason it's here is not to tell the truth.

Quieting the Inner Critic

In this book, I'm going to show you how to quiet the inner critic. How to get its annoying, nagging voice to lower to a whisper and maybe even disappear completely. Contrary to what you might think, it doesn't happen by just hitting it over the head with a sledgehammer, as tempting as that might be. It takes practice, and the courage to learn a new set of skills and believe that they can work, and then more practice, practice, practice.

We learn to quiet the inner critic through a set of skills called self-compassion. Self-compassion works *with* the inner critic, so that it gets smaller and weaker, and sometimes even seems to have disappeared into the woodwork.

What Is Self-Compassion Anyway?

What are we talking about when we talk about self-compassion? Self-compassion is about being kind to ourselves when we're having a hard time, when something happens that makes us feel really awful. We know what compassion is—we've heard about compassion our whole lives. Compassion is about being kind and caring to others, particularly when they're struggling. Self-compassion, then, is turning that kindness and caring toward ourselves. I know, that may sound like selfishness or self-indulgence. But truthfully— and we know this from research—when we're kinder to ourselves, we are better able to be kind toward others. We have more to give.

People often think that we have to beat ourselves up in order to work hard and achieve our goals. But research has shown that this isn't true—that when we are nicer to ourselves, we actually work harder. Knowing that we won't say nasty things to ourselves if we fail, we're more likely to take chances, be creative, try new things. We actually are *more* motivated when we are kind to ourselves. And there's no limit to compassion—just because we're giving more to ourselves, that doesn't mean that we have less to give to others. Quite the opposite. And one more thing—most of us are nicer to our friends when they're having a bad day than we are to ourselves. So know that if this describes you, you are not alone!

There are three parts to self-compassion: mindfulness, common humanity, and self-kindness. Mindfulness is noticing what's happening—your feelings, physical sensations, and thoughts—in the moment that they're happening. It's about having a balanced perspective and not freaking out when things aren't going the way that we'd like them to, because we know that whatever is happening isn't going to last forever. Common humanity is understanding that what we're going through is simply part of being human, and something we all experience. And self-kindness is just what it sounds like—being kind to ourselves, especially when we most need it.

Don't worry, I'll explain these parts in more detail in the next few chapters. The skills that you will learn in this book focus on one, two, or all three of these components—and they'll help you deal with not only that annoying inner critic, but also the day-to-day tough spots that you run into being a teen.

About Me

Before we launch ahead, I thought you might want to know a little about me. I'm a researcher and university professor who studies how being self-compassionate can help teens better deal with stress. I ask questions like: What happens when teens are more self-compassionate? How does being less self-compassionate hurt them? What can help teens be more self-compassionate? And then I conduct research studies to answer those questions.

With my colleague Lorraine Hobbs, I adapted an adult self-compassion program created by Dr. Kristin Neff and Dr. Chris Germer, to make it more interesting for teens. The teen program is called "Making Friends with Yourself: A Mindful Self-Compassion Program for Teens." We've published a couple research studies on this program showing that it reduces stress for teens—and in some cases, also reduces anxiety and depression. A version of the program can also be used in classrooms.

Many other researchers around the world are now studying this program (which we call MFY for short), and there will likely be more research on it in the near future. Many of the practices and exercises in this book are adapted from both adult Mindful Self-Compassion program and the teen Making Friends with Yourself program. My book *The Self-Compassion Workbook for Teens: Mindfulness and Compassion Skills to Overcome Self-Criticism and Embrace Who You Are*, published a few years ago, provides mindfulness and self-compassion skills for teens. This book takes that one step further: putting those skills into action by showing how they can be used to deal with stressors that teens face every day, like school, social media, self-image, and issues around gender and sexuality.

Navigating This Book

In part 1, you'll read about what self-compassion is and how it can help you quiet the inner critic and strengthen your own true voice. This can give you the power to deal with the general stress and feelings of inadequacy that go along with being a teen. In part 2, you'll read about how to address specific stressors that most teens face at one time or another—and ways to put self-compassion into action in your daily life.

Both formal and informal self-compassion practices will be offered throughout. With formal practices, you will set aside time each day (five or ten minutes) and sit down to do a guided meditation or an exercise. Informal practices are "in the moment." When something happens that upsets you, you can jump into one of these practices right then and there—they only take a minute or two. They will provide you with the direct experience of being kind to yourself, so that you'll know how to do it when you need it later on.

Dive in and learn about self-compassion and how it will help you not only lessen that inner critical voice, but also be more effective and successful in your life.

CHAPTER 1

Mindfulness, or How to Hear Your Own True Voice

Maybe you've heard about mindfulness. The word has been thrown around quite a bit lately in the media—there are even a bunch of mindfulness apps for your phone that provide everything from guided meditations to music to help you fall asleep. Put simply, mindfulness means paying attention to what's happening right in this very moment, with an attitude of curiosity and interest. It means noticing what you're feeling as you're feeling it.

This is an essential component of self-compassion, because in order to be kind to ourselves, we need to know what we're feeling. We need to be aware of all of it—the angry feelings, the hurt feelings, the feelings of being not good enough. We open up to everything that's arising—all the feelings, thoughts, and physical sensations coming up in each moment.

Importantly, this means being aware of everything, kind of like a scientist would—observing from the outside.

Perhaps you notice a rush of anger, for example. You might then say to yourself, *Hmm, this is anger. What a strong feeling this is! It feels like it wants to overtake me and run the show.* Or it might mean noticing a self-critical thought, like *Wow, you really messed up that history presentation. Why didn't you practice more? You looked like an idiot in front of the whole class!*

You might be thinking, *Terrific. I'm freaking out about college applications and the SAT already—how is noticing how anxious I am going to help? Seems like it will make me feel worse!"*

There isn't much we can do about the boatload of applications teens have to complete to get into college, or the insane amount of academic pressure put on teens today, which creates a ton of anxiety and depression. Yes, society and our educational system need to address this huge problem. Until something changes, mindfulness can help. Here's how.

• *Dominic's Story*

Dominic, a senior in a public school in a large city, took a mindfulness course last year that was offered in his high school. He now practices mindfulness about ten to fifteen minutes a day, and has found that it really helps him not get so stressed. For example, rather than freaking out or getting super anxious, Dominic takes each task one at a time: first one college application, then the next college application, then maybe next week a practice SAT test. Dominic moves about the tasks in his life without a lot of emotional upheaval. That's not to say he never gets anxious—we all get anxious at times—but Dominic has learned to manage his stress in a healthy way.

He has noticed that when anxiety starts creeping in, his heart starts to beat more rapidly, his breathing speeds up, and his body tenses. At this point, whenever possible, he stops and simply notices these sensations, almost like an outsider observing them.

He notices his anxious thoughts, like Am I ever going to be able to finish these applications? *or* What's going to happen to me if I don't get into college? *Like all of us, he has a choice—he can get hooked by these negative thoughts and start obsessing about them, or he can simply let them pass, which is what Dominic has learned to do. When these thoughts arise, he simply notices them and lets them drift by—like watching clouds drift across the sky. He knows that his thoughts aren't facts—just because he thinks them, that doesn't mean they're true. They are simply expressing a part of him that is fearful.*

Each time the anxious thoughts arise, Dominic comes back to his anchor—the physical sensations of his feet on the floor. In this way, he is taking away the power of his anxious thoughts by not getting swept away by them or letting them control him.

By paying attention in this way, Dominic has learned to live his life with a lot of ease and a minimal amount of anxiety and fear, and he has a lot more energy to tackle the mountain of academic tasks ahead of him.

What Happens When We Pay Attention

When we pay attention to our thoughts, feelings, and physical sensations, we notice some interesting things—such as how our mind frequently wanders. This is often one of the first things we notice when we start to practice mindfulness. We might be thinking one thought one minute, and the next minute we're thinking of something else, and then that evolves to another thought, and then another subject entirely. Our minds tend to obsess or ruminate about certain situations in our lives, like they're playing the same film clip over and over.

Mindfulness practice teaches us to notice when our mind has wandered, and then gently guide our attention back to what's here in the present moment—our thoughts, feelings, and physical sensations. When we are able to keep our attention in the present moment, we can more easily hear our own true voice, and we're less distracted by the fears and anxiety circling around in our minds.

Let's see if we can investigate mind-wandering a little more, by trying a mindful breathing practice.

Practice: Mindful Breathing...With a Little Compassion

You can download audio for this meditation at http://www.newharbinger.com/45274.

This practice can be done either informally—right in the moment, when you notice that you're feeling stressed—or formally, with a few minutes set aside for it. Either way, it will work.

First, find a place to sit where you can get comfortable and won't be interrupted. If you're okay with it, go ahead and close your eyes.

- Find a point where you can easily notice your breathing—inside your nostrils as the air passes through, or at your lips or tip of your nose as you're breathing out, or in the up and down movement of your chest. Or in the movement of your diaphragm, right below your rib cage, as it moves in and out with each breath.

- Now, just feel your breath: as you breathe in and as you breathe out. Notice the whole length of your breath, from the very start of your in-breath to the end of your out-breath. You may even notice a pause at the end of your in-breath, before the start of your out-breath, and a pause at the end of your out-breath, before the next in-breath starts.

- One breath. Then the next breath. And the next.

- At some point, you'll notice that your mind has wandered, and you're thinking about something. This could be something that's coming up in school, something going on with a friend, or just some random thought like what you're going to do after school.

- Not a problem! This is part of the practice. Just gently bring your attention back to your breath.

- You might sense that the air you breathe in is nurturing you, taking oxygen to your lungs and then heart and bringing oxygenated blood to every cell in your body. The air you breathe in is taking care of you! You might imagine how it comes in, fills your lungs, moves to your heart, and then travels throughout your body, even to the very tips of your toes and fingers.

- As you breathe out—and it helps if you can make your out-breath a little longer than your in-breath—notice how your body relaxes. Your belly extends, your shoulders drop, your chest sinks in a little, and you might notice that your body drops a little more deeply into the chair.

- Each time you notice that you're thinking, just gently, without scolding yourself (no need for that!), return your attention to your breath. When you're ready, open your eyes if they've been closed.

That's it! It's that simple. You can do this either for just three breaths, as an informal practice, or for a longer formal practice.

Did you notice your mind wandering when you were paying attention to your breathing? My guess is that you did. Our minds wander because they are searching for anything that can hurt us, so they can protect us, and so we're not caught off guard. For example, you may notice your mind returning to the same story—maybe an assignment that is due soon that you're worried about. Your mind is constantly reminding you of the assignment, to make sure that you don't forget about it and get an F. Our minds are like security guards, constantly surveying the scenery to make sure we're safe.

Our Minds at Work

This is what our minds are wired to do. They try to protect us by getting us ready for what needs to be done. They are on the lookout for us, and they get us ready just in case the situation presents itself again. Next time, we'll have that perfect comeback. Next time, we won't be left feeling unheard or unsafe.

Here's an example: you're walking down the hall at school. There are a group of popular kids hanging out by the stairs, and as you walk by they look at you and then turn to each other and start to laugh. You don't know what to say, because you don't know what's going on, so you just hurry by.

What goes on in your head? Maybe you start thinking that you should have defended yourself. Maybe you wonder what they may have been saying to each other. You might feel embarrassed, maybe a little ashamed, and wonder what it is about you that they were laughing at. Was it something about your clothes? Is there some gossip circulating about you? Did you have food on your face from lunch?

Your mind is searching—wandering—for answers, and thinking about how you should have handled it, and how you could do it differently next time. So that next time, you can walk away with your head held high. So you won't be hurt. It keeps going back to this scenario because it's working to figure out ways to protect you. That's its job. We're biologically set up that way.

Imagine being a nomad out in the wilderness, hunting and gathering. If you didn't stay alert to things out there that might hurt you—a bear searching for food, for example— you might be eaten by that bear. We've survived as a species by keeping a lookout for the things that could harm us. Unfortunately, in today's world, when things are more likely to harm us emotionally than physically, this ancient system doesn't work so well. We get stuck in dwelling on what the popular kids were whispering about in the hallway.

The Problem with the Wandering Mind

What's wrong with replaying stories of things that we've gone through and are struggling to understand?

For one, if our minds are filled with stories about things that happened in the past—or things that we're worried may happen in the future—we aren't aware of what's happening *now*. If our minds are somewhere else, we're likely to miss certain cues occurring in the present moment. Which means if we're in a tense basketball game, chances are we're not going to make that critical game-winning basket. If we're taking an algebra test, we're not going to be able to figure out what x or y equal. And if we're playing the piano, we might miss that complicated trill, because we're not actually paying attention to what's going on in with our fingers.

The other problem with our minds revisiting these problem scenarios is that we know from research that when we obsess over something that happened, we are more likely to be depressed. And when we worry about the future, we tend to be more anxious. So our minds are biologically geared to help us survive, but not necessarily to help us be happy.

And more than that, all that noise in our head—all that ruminating and worrying—prevents us from hearing our own true voice. That voice deep down in the core of our being that knows us very well and knows what's best for us, and loves us completely and unconditionally. This voice is very wise, but sometimes hard to hear amidst all the other voices. Those other voices—the ruminating voice, the worrying

15

voice, the inner critic voice—can be really loud. In order to hear our own true voice, we need to quiet the other voices.

The Solution: Hearing Your Own True Voice

So how do we do this? For one, we can practice not dwelling in the past or the future. This is where mindfulness practice comes in.

Mindfulness teaches us how to be here with what's happening in the present moment. Rather than our minds swimming in a pool of past and future thoughts, we focus on what we're feeling right now, in this moment. This is what Dominic was doing in the beginning of the chapter. He was letting go of the fearful "what-ifs" and bringing his attention to what was happening right in the moment—sounds in the room, his breath, or physical sensations. That way he was in a place where he could give himself what he needed. If he was being self-critical, for example, Dominic could give himself self-compassion.

Doing this is actually quite simple. We focus on physical sensations—which always take place in the present moment. We notice the feeling of our feet on the floor. Or our breath as we breathe in and out. Or the feeling of an object in our hand. Or the sensations of our lips touching each other. Or a million other physical sensations. Really, any physical sensation will do.

Here are a couple of mindfulness practices that you can do anywhere, to help you clear out the worrying, ruminating, self-critical voices so that our calmer, clearer voice can come through.

This first one is called "Soles of the Feet," and we have Nirbhay Singh to thank for this practice. He brought it to our attention in an article he published in 2003. It's been modified for the Mindful Self-Compassion program, and I've modified it a bit further here.

Exercise: Soles of the Feet

You can download audio for this exercise at http://www.newharbinger.com/45274.

This is best to do in bare feet or socks. It's okay to do with shoes on, but definitely try it with shoes off at some point. When your mind wanders, simply come back to the feeling in the soles of the feet.

- Stand up and notice the feeling of your body as you are simply standing. Notice the weight of your body on your feet, and how your body feels in space.

- Now notice the feeling of your soles on the floor. Does the floor feel hard against your feet? Is there a bit of cushion? Do the bottoms of your feet feel warm? Cool? What other sensations do you notice?

- Rock forward half an inch. What do you notice? What changes on the bottoms of your feet?

- Now come back to center and lean back half an inch. What do you notice now?

- Lean forward again just a little, noticing what's happening on the bottoms of your feet. Now lean back a little, noticing any change in sensation. Try this a few times, slowly, paying attention to what's happening on the soles of your feet.

- Now try leaning just a little bit—a half inch—to the left. Notice how sensations change on the bottoms of your feet.

- Now lean a little to the right—a half inch. Again, notice what's changing.

- Lean slightly to the left and then to the right. As you do, notice the changing sensations.

- You may notice how the bottoms of your feet are small, relative to the rest of your body, yet they support your entire body all day long. Perhaps take a moment to appreciate all the work your feet do for you. Maybe even be thankful that you have feet, because not everyone does.

- Take another moment to feel the weight of your body as you're standing here, and when you feel ready, sit down again.

You may have noticed that when you're focused on a physical sensation, like the soles of your feet, you are less stressed and anxious, because you're focused on the present moment. Our minds aren't jumping to the future, where our anxiety lies—like worrying about getting into college. When we stay in the present moment—as much as we are able—we're less stressed.

Here's another practice to help quiet your mind, so that you can decrease stress and build the courage to be yourself. If you're the kind of person who has trouble being still and likes to move, you might like this one.

Exercise: Mindful Movement

You can download audio for this exercise at http://www.newharbinger.com/45274.

- Start by standing upright, with your arms relaxed at your sides. Notice how your body feels as you stand still, motionless.

- Now, very slowly, move your body however feels good to you. As you move, notice the sensations in your muscles. For example, if you are stretching your arms above you, notice how your arms feel as you reach toward the sky.

Here are some suggestions of ways to move that feel good and are fun. Try any or all of them and see which you like best.

1. Rag Doll

Lean over from your waist so that your arms, head, and shoulders drop in front of you, with your hands reaching toward the floor. You can bend your knees so that your belly comes close to touching your legs. Your hands don't have to touch the floor—they can just hang there or you can hold your elbows with either hand.

Just relax and let yourself hang. If you like, you can sway a little, front to back or side to side.

Now pretend someone has a string around your waist and is hovering above you on the ceiling, slowly pulling the string, so that your waist is lifting slowly, bit by bit, your back raising one vertebra at a time.

Finally, your shoulders raise up, then your neck, and finally your head.

2. The Belly Dancer

Stand with your hands on your hips, and take a moment to notice how you feel. How do your feet feel on the floor? How does your body feel in space? How do your hands feel on your hips?

Make circles with your hips slowly in one direction, keeping everything above your waist as still as possible. As you move in these slow circles, notice any sensations or movements in your legs—your upper legs, knees, lower legs, and even your feet. What changes by simply moving your hips?

Now try the hip circles in the opposite direction. Any difference from what happened when you circled in the other direction?

Now shake your hips, any way you'd like. Imagine that there are all kinds of bells hanging from your hips, making noise. Shake them however you'd like, making as much noise as you can. What do you notice? What do you feel in your hips? Legs? Knees? Feet?

Now come back to stillness, where you started—feet planted on the ground, hands on your hips. Notice what you're feeling right now. Any sense of energy moving through the body? Any vibrations? Or maybe you don't feel anything at all?

Remember, whatever you feel or don't feel—it's fine. You're not supposed to feel anything in particular—it's the paying attention that's important.

3. The Juggler

This time, imagine you're a master juggler. Pretend that you have a feather, a bowling pin, and a tennis ball. Toss the feather in the air, watch it as it floats down—and before you catch it, toss the bowling pin.

Grab the feather, toss the tennis ball, and quickly grab the bowling pin before launching the feather again.

Continue in this way—feather, bowling pin, tennis ball. If you drop one, it's fine! Just pick it up and continue to practice juggling.

4. **The Cat/The Cow**

This one will likely be most comfortable on a rug or yoga mat. Get on all fours, with your hands placed on the floor and under your shoulders, and your knees hip distance apart. Make sure your head and neck are aligned with your spine. This is called tabletop position, because your back is like a tabletop. Notice how you feel resting in this position, any sensations you feel in your body. Pay attention to the sensation of your breath as you breathe in, feeling the air moving into your nose, filling your lungs, and moving out of your body on the exhale.

On the next inhale, arch your back, noticing how your hips, shoulders, neck, and head move naturally upward with the arch of your back. This is called the cow pose, because it looks like a cow grazing in a field (okay, maybe that's a bit of a stretch, no pun intended!).

On the exhale, round your back as the air moves out of your lungs, noticing how the shoulders, neck, and crown of the head naturally move downward toward the floor. This is called cat pose, because it's like a cat stretching her back.

Repeat the cat and cow poses several times at your own pace, noticing the different sensations in your body—the stretching of muscles in your back, shoulders, and hips. When you notice thoughts arising in your mind (which they will), simply bring your attention back to feeling sensations in your body. Each time you notice your mind wandering as you do cat/cow, simply bring your attention back to the physical sensations.

Conclusion

When you were doing these mindful movements, and paying attention to the sensations, did you notice that you weren't anxious or having self-critical thoughts? That's because you were caught up in feeling the physical sensations. You were in the present moment!

When this happens—and even if it happens only for a split second, it counts—you're being mindful. Part of being mindful means that you are able to locate your feelings where they appear in your body, so, when you notice difficult feelings arise, you can practice self-compassion.

Congratulations! You can revisit these exercises anytime. You're on the road to becoming more self-compassionate!

Next, we're going to check out the second component of self-compassion: common humanity.

CHAPTER 2

Common Humanity—
You Are Not Alone!

Jamie felt alone. Her parents were going through an awful divorce, and as a result she had recently moved to a new town where she knew no one. She was miserable. She spent most of her time in her room, on her phone, messaging her friends from her old school—which didn't make her feel any better, because they were hanging out, doing fun things together, and here she was, in this apartment with her dad and his new girlfriend. The classes were all different at her new school; her grades were taking a nosedive because she had no idea what was going on. She felt lost. Everyone had their cliques, and she wasn't in any of them—it seemed like everyone had known each other since kindergarten. Worst of all, no one seemed to understand or care about what she was going through.

You may often feel like you are all alone—that no one else feels what you do. You may be haunted with feelings of insecurity and worthlessness. Sometimes things seem okay—sometimes you actually feel happy—but then the next moment, you're sobbing and you have no idea why.

This feeling of loneliness and feeling "not enough" is compounded by social media. As we know, people present the best sides of themselves on social media—not the real stuff they're going through every day, but often only what makes them look good. The impression that you often get is that others' lives are simply fantastic. They're not struggling. Their lives are going along fabulously, without even a tiny bump in the road. So, you might conclude that something must really be wrong with you—that you're the only one having such a hard time.

We live in an image-oriented society, driven by advertising and the quest for profit. It can be hard not to feel isolated in the modern world. Add to that the fact that social comparison is just what we do as humans—and it's particularly rampant in the teen years.

End result: You have looming feelings of unworthiness, often feel "less than," and to top it off, you're sure that you're the only idiot who feels that way. Everyone else has their life together.

Yet common humanity offers another outlook—something completely different.

What Is Common Humanity?

Common humanity is the understanding that the emotions we experience—sadness, hurt, frustration, anger, and even crushing despair—are part of the experience of being human. Common humanity is the component of self-compassion that tells us that what we feel and experience is normal and to be expected. Just like we feel joy, excitement, pleasure, and love, we are also faced with the other side of emotions—those "negative" emotions. This is how it works to be human—we feel the full range of emotions, from the very greatest pleasure to the deepest despair. And the other two components of self-compassion—mindfulness and self-kindness—help us to be aware of these emotions and to know what to do with them.

We all feel the range of emotions, including all the negative ones. Some of us choose to fight the bad feelings, resist them, or hide them from others (or even from ourselves), and others prefer to share their feelings with friends or family. Regardless, we all experience them.

Common humanity is remembering that we are not alone—that we are one person out of the 7.7 billion roaming around on this planet who experience hurt, grief, disappointment, depression, and anxiety. So, although Jamie, in the story at the beginning of the chapter, might *feel* alone, and when she looks around everyone may *appear* to be ecstatically happy and never feeling a single negative feeling, the reality is that we all struggle. Others may be hiding it well, but the struggle and challenges are there.

It can help to remember that we all struggle.

Why Is Common Humanity So Important?

Understanding common humanity helps us remember that we are not alone, that others struggle as well, and that this is all part of being human. You might be wondering why it's so important for us to realize this—to feel connected to others, to feel like we fit in.

Simply put, it's basic to our biology. From an evolutionary standpoint, we need others to survive. We need others to help us take care of our offspring—and to produce offspring! In prehistoric times, staying together in groups had protective benefits, especially when hunting large animals or guarding the tribe against possible attacks by outsiders. Particularly when food was scarce, someone with the protection of a group was more likely to get food than someone who was a lone wolf, trying to survive on their own.

It's important to recognize that this message—this need to connect with others—is embedded in our biology. We need others to survive. So if you're thinking that maybe there's something wrong with you for wanting to be part of a group or wanting friends, trust me, it's nothing to be ashamed of—it's true for all of us.

Here's an exercise that will help you remember that we all experience the full range of emotions. In this exercise, you will be bringing to mind someone you know. I recommend trying this exercise a couple of times with different people—a good friend, a family member, maybe someone who annoys you, or maybe the super popular kid at school. Maybe even someone who you look up to and follow on social media. You'll get different results for different people. Treat it like an experiment!

Exercise: A Person Just like Me

You can download audio for this exercise at
http://www.newharbinger.com/45274.

This practice is credited to Trish Broderick, who adapted it from the work of Chade-Meng Tan, to use in her Learning to BREATHE teen mindfulness curriculum.

This exercise asks you to visualize something in your mind, and it's usually easier to visualize when your eyes are closed. Close your eyes if you're comfortable doing so, and take a few deep breaths to allow yourself to settle and relax a bit.

As you breathe, see if you can let go a little more, with each out-breath, of any tension or stress in your body. Simply relaxing. Simply letting go.

Now bring to mind a person you know. This can be someone you know well, or some random person in one of your classes—maybe someone you've been curious about, or it could even be someone who you've never really thought anything about one way or the other. If you're up for a challenge, you can even choose someone who really bugs you—maybe that kid in your class whose hand shoots up every time the teacher asks a question, or maybe a younger brother or sister. Or, it can be someone who you admire but haven't met personally—like someone on a Netflix series or someone you follow on social media.

I'm going to ask you to repeat the following phrases slowly to yourself as you think of that person. It's really important that you don't rush through them, but take your time so that they really sink in. As you say them, think about their meaning. You can replace "this person" with their name.

- Let's consider a few things about this person:
  - *"This person is a human being, just like me."*
  - *"This person has a body and a mind, just like me."*
  - *"This person has feelings, emotions, and thoughts, just like me."*
  - *"This person has, at some point, been sad, disappointed, angry, hurt, and confused, just like me."*
  - *"This person wishes to be free from pain and unhappiness, just like me."*
  - *"This person wishes to be safe, healthy, and loved, just like me."*
  - *"This person wishes to be happy, just like me."*

- Now let's allow some wishes for this person to arise:

  - *"I wish for this person to have the strength, resources, and support to help him or her through the difficult times in life."*

  - *"I wish for this person to be free from pain and suffering."*

  - *"I wish for this person to be strong and balanced."*

  - *"I wish for this person to be happy, because this person is a fellow human being, just like me."*

- *Take a few deep breaths and notice what you're feeling.*

You may notice some surprises when doing this exercise. If you did it for a good friend, perhaps you feel a little bit closer to them, a little more tenderness or understanding. Maybe you feel like your heart is opening a little more toward them. If you did it for a famous person that you've looked up to and never met, perhaps you were surprised by what came up for you—maybe the realization that they also are very much human, and have feelings and hurts and disappointments. And if you did it for that person who really annoys you—which, by the way, can be really challenging to do—were you surprised by the fact that this person struggles too and is just trying to find their way, like the rest of us?

This is a great practice to do regularly for people in your life—particularly when you're having a hard time with someone. It helps you to see that they are human and, as such, they struggle too. Sometimes they mess up, have conflicts with others, stumble and fall—and, like you and the rest of us, somehow they manage to pick themselves up and continue on their life journey. Picking yourself up and going on is not an easy thing to do, and certainly takes courage. But it also allows you to figure out who you are and what you need to be happy.

Core Values—We All Have Them

Another thing that connects us with all humans across the planet is that we all have core values. Core values are the things that we believe in, that are meaningful to us, that guide us around how we want to live our lives. Core values live deep in our core—they are basic to who we are as people. They differ from person to person. Examples of core values are education, relationships with family and friends, faith, being outdoors, traveling and exploring the world, listening or playing music, and creating art.

In order to know how to be self-compassionate, it's helpful to know what our core values are. That way, when we're stuck and confused about which way to go with a decision that we have to make, we can come back to our core values. Also, because we are social beings, we may be influenced by others, or even find ourselves living in a way that might not be in agreement with—or, worse, go against—our core values. When this happens, we can feel disoriented, stressed, and upset with ourselves, and our self-critical voice can emerge. Knowing what our core values are can orient our lives and guide our actions.

But how can we identify our core values? Here is a reflective exercise that uses a house as a metaphor for your life, and can help you to discover your core values. This exercise can be found in the teen self-compassion program Making Friends with Yourself, which was inspired by a similar exercise for adults in the Mindful Self-Compassion program developed by Chris Germer and Kristin Neff.

Exercise: My House/My Self

Part 1: Imagine a House

You can draw a picture of a house if you'd like, or simply imagine one in your mind. Make sure your house has a garden, a chimney, a fence, a foundation, and windows, and is made of brick.

As you answer the questions below, related to the parts of the house, take time to reflect upon your responses. You'll probably notice that your answers to several of the questions are similar—don't worry about that. Know that you can interpret the questions however you like. The point is to really take the time to think about each question. It's best to write the answers down as you go.

1. Foundation. What things are foundational to you—your most important values?

2. Window. When you look out the window of your house into the future, what do you see?

3. Path to front door. What are the things that lead you to your house—the things that you believe in?

4. Garden. What kinds of things would you like to grow or cultivate in your life?

5. Interior. Who are the people who have influenced you in your life?

6. Chimney. What parts of yourself would you like to release into the world?

7. Fence. What things do you want to keep away from your house?

8. Roof. What keeps you inside? What is limiting you?

9. Bricks. What holds you together?

If you would like to add something to your house, please feel free to do so.

After finishing part one, you probably have a pretty good idea of what you value, what you'd like to keep and cultivate in your life, as well as what you'd like to let go of, or keep out of your life. You might also have noticed that although some things are really important to you, you don't spend much time or energy on them. For example, you might really love being outside playing sports, but realize that you don't spend much time doing that. This is true for most of us—we all get frustrated when we aren't living the way we'd like to.

Often, this disconnect occurs because there are obstacles standing in the way of us living according to our core values. Frustration around not living the way we'd like to is another element of our common humanity, something we all have in common at certain times in our lives. In Part 2 of this exercise, you'll explore these obstacles—both external and internal.

Part 2: Obstacles

External obstacles. Frequently, external factors stand in the way of us living by our values. For example, you may really want to explore the world, but not have the money or time to do that. Or you may really want to spend time hanging out with friends, but live too far away from them to walk and don't yet have a driver's license or a car. Or you may want to go to art school, and have parents who think that's a waste of time and that you should study something more academic—like biology or statistics.

- Take some time now to think about whether there are any external obstacles standing in the way of you living by your values. Go ahead and write these down.

Internal obstacles. Internal obstacles are things like fear of failure, or being really hard on yourself, or thinking that you don't deserve happiness. Perhaps you'd like to spend more time reading fantasy novels, but you feel pressured to continually check in on social media—on some level, you have FOMO —fear of missing out. Or maybe you want to try out for the school musical, but are afraid that your singing isn't good enough. Or you'd like to ask someone out, but are too afraid they'll say no. So you never ask anyone. Ever.

- Take a few moments and think about whether there are any internal obstacles standing in the way of you living how you'd like to live. You can be honest with yourself, because no one else is listening—it's just you and your own true voice. Take a moment to write down these internal obstacles.

- If you identified any obstacles, can you say some kind words to yourself, acknowledging that it's challenging, not being able to live according to your values? Perhaps you can tell yourself, "This is hard! But it won't be forever—everything changes." Maybe you've been self-critical because you tend to go along with the crowd, and not stand by or live by your core values. If this is the case, write down some kind words to yourself, the words that you might say to a friend. Maybe something like "It's really hard to stand up for yourself, and to say no to your friends when you know you should be doing your homework." Maybe you can say something like "All teens go through this! It's natural to feel pressure to go along with the crowd!" Or perhaps, "What I've done in the past is the past, and I can't change it. But maybe in the future I can live the way I want to live and be more comfortable with myself."

- And maybe the obstacle is simply that you're human, and being human, you can't be perfect. If this is the case, can you forgive yourself for not being perfect? Maybe you can say something to yourself like, "No one is perfect! It's totally fine to struggle sometimes, and forget about my core values and go along with the crowd—in fact, it's human!"

Exercise: Making a Pledge to Yourself

Sometimes it's helpful to reorient yourself when you've drifted away from your core values. Imagine that one day you find yourself immersed in a social media site (or two or three) and wrapped up in this whirlwind of comparing yourself with others, and you're feeling awful. Worst of all, a whole afternoon has gone by, and you realize you could have been doing something else—something that actually makes you feel good. Creating a pledge can help keep you on track for next time—to remember what's important to you, and live in accordance with that.

- Take a moment to choose one of your core values that is really important to you. Create a pledge to yourself by writing down "I pledge to [core value here] as best I can." Remember that a pledge isn't the same as a rule or a contract—a pledge simply states that you are making an effort to live by this value. Like all of us humans, you will likely forget and there will be days that you don't follow your pledge. When this happens, no need to beat yourself up—simply reorient yourself to it.

To help you remember your pledge, you can post it somewhere after writing it out. If it isn't too personal, you could take a picture of it and make it the background on your phone. Or you can put it on your dresser, where you'll see it every day—to remember when you go astray.

Conclusion

Common humanity is understanding that our emotional struggles are not unique to us, but part of being human and living on this planet. Although it often feels like we are alone—especially when we're consumed with hurt, anger, or frustration—common humanity reminds us that this is what human beings experience: emotional ups and downs, times when things are going well, and times when it feels like things couldn't get worse. Knowing that these challenges aren't our fault, but just part of being alive and human, can help to relieve some of the pain.

Core values—and the struggles we face when we stray from them—are examples of common humanity. We all struggle when obstacles keep us from living by our core values. At these moments, we can open the door to treating ourselves with kindness. The next chapter will help you learn how to do this.

CHAPTER 3

Self-Kindness—
Treating Yourself like
You'd Treat a Good Friend

Kai leaves the lunch line and scans the school cafeteria for a place to sit. There she is, the cute girl he's crushing on, chatting with her friends. And...there's an empty seat next to her!

He takes a breath, gathers up all the confidence he can muster, and confidently (at least it appears that way) walks over, sitting down next to her.

She looks up from her conversation, he smiles, and she says, "I'm saving that seat for someone."

Kai mumbles an apology, awkwardly gathers his things, and finds his way to another table. His inner critic is screaming in his ear, *Total fail! And everyone saw it! Who do you think you are, anyway? You really think she'd want to sit with you when she could have anyone in this school? You're pathetic!* He plasters a cool expression on his face, but inside that inner critic won't stop its relentless assault, and his heart sinks into his chest.

What to do? Kai wishes he could make that negative voice in him disappear—or better yet, make himself disappear. Instead, Kai remembers his mindfulness skills. He feels the soles of his feet in his shoes, and the stickiness of the cafeteria floor under his running shoes. He takes a breath and feels his breath passing into his nostrils, filling his lungs; he feels his lungs expand, then lets go, releasing his breath as his shoulders and chest relax. *Just stay with your breath,* he tells himself, *one breath at a time.*

As Kai continues to use these skills, his breath and the sensations in his body take center stage in his mind, and the self-critic fades into the background.

What just happened? Well, in a nutshell, Kai was hurting—but by being mindful, he was able to care for himself, giving himself what he needed. By focusing on what was actually present right now in this moment, through physical sensations, he was able to let go of the "story" racing through his mind—the voice telling him he was a jerk. End result: Less embarrassment, less anxiety, and a sense of being supported.

Notice that Kai didn't shut the voice out, or stick his fingers in his ears and scream, "La, la, la, I'm not listening!" Why? Why doesn't it work to simply tell that irritating voice to go away and leave us alone?

The reason is this: The inner critic is a part of us. It's here to try to keep us safe and to protect us. When it was screaming at Kai at the lunch table, it was trying to tell him—in maybe not the most helpful way—to protect himself from getting hurt. It wants us to be the best we can be, but its methods are a little harsh and unrelenting—and it can drown out your own true voice.

Dealing with the Inner Critic

So what can you do when your inner critic blabs on and on? Here's an idea that really works.

First of all, picture your inner critic in your mind. What do they look like? How do they dress? How do they walk? What does their voice sound like? What are their facial features? Get a really clear image of your inner critic in your mind. It also helps to name them.

Next, imagine a little room in your head, kind of like a small doctor's waiting room, with couches and chairs all around. Welcome your inner critic into this room, using their name if you want, and let them have a seat. Explain to your inner critic that you understand that they have been trying to protect you for many years, and while you appreciate their efforts, you're not going to listen to them anymore. They can talk to you as much as they want, but you don't have to listen to them, or follow their orders.

My inner critic is named Marsha, because she reminds me of a Marsha on an old TV show who was kind of bratty. So, I might say, "Hi, Marsha, come on in! Have a seat. You can sit here and hang out, but I don't have to listen to you." Then I smile and walk away.

So we let the inner critic in, because they usually mean no harm, and really are just trying to protect us—in Kai's case, it's protecting Kai from getting embarrassed again. If there were no inner critic, Kai might keep finding himself in situations where he's not welcome, and each time might feel embarrassed, which could really wear him down. Yes, the inner critic often goes over the top and gets a little mean—too much of which can make you anxious or depressed. But here's the secret: Marsha can blab away all she wants. I don't have to pay any attention to her. She's just a voice in my head, and she is not speaking my truth. Just because we're thinking something doesn't mean that it's true. Contrary to popular belief, our thoughts are not facts.

As a meditation teacher once said, thoughts are only "secretions from our brain" (ew) with little or no connection to what's happening in the real world. So although our thoughts—the voice of the inner critic, for example—might have a kernel of truth embedded somewhere in them, the inner critical voice is most certainly not speaking the whole truth.

Getting Space from Things that Hurt Us

Self-kindness allows you to create distance from things that hurt you, such as the inner critic. Self-kindness means being brave enough and respecting yourself enough to stand up for yourself. This could mean not listening to your inner critic all the time, or it could mean letting go of friends that hurt your feelings, not watching movies that make you feel afraid, or not paying attention to social media that makes you feel bad. (In some cases, it might mean letting go of social media altogether.) It could also mean confronting people or standing up for yourself when you feel like you're being mistreated. In a nutshell, self-kindness is about treating yourself with the respect and kindness that you deserve.

Self-kindness is one way to make changes in your life that are good for you—that will help you grow into the person you want to be. Here's an exercise that will help you learn how to be kinder to yourself. It was inspired by a Mindful Self-Compassion guided meditation.

Exercise: Visualize Meeting Your Inner Critic... and Someone Else

You can download audio for this exercise at http://www.newharbinger.com/45274.

First, get into a comfortable position, either sitting or lying down. Take a few deep, relaxing breaths, allowing yourself to let go a little more with each out-breath, letting your body sink deeper into the chair or floor as you breathe out.

In your mind, create a room that feels very safe. You can bring in whatever you'd like for decor—some comfy chairs, a few pillows, sports trophies, your favorite books, perhaps a few things from your room at home. You can relax in this room however you'd like—maybe flopping down on a bean bag, sitting on your bed, or lounging on a couch. Whatever makes you feel comfortable and relaxed. Take some time to simply enjoy being in the space, with all your favorite things, feeling safe, secure, and protected, warm and cozy.

Now imagine that you hear a knock at the door. You recognize your inner critic standing on the other side of the door; knowing that the inner critic is only here to protect you, you reach for the doorknob and let her in. As soon as she steps over the threshold of the door, she shrinks a little, becomes a little smaller and a little weaker. You notice that her arms suddenly seem shriveled, and where there were once muscles, now there's only skin. You feel compassion for your inner critic because she's been with you for such a long time, and you know that despite the fact that you've been hurt by her quite a bit, she's meant well. So you tell her to take a seat, which she does, sitting primly on a chair.

Before you get a chance to sit down, you hear another knock at the door. You go to the door, put your hand on the knob, wondering who it could be this time. As you open the door, this time the guest looks vaguely familiar. You recognize their face but can't remember from where. As you let them in, you're struck by the kindness exuding from this person. As this mystery guest steps across the threshold of your space, you immediately feel an outpouring of love that fills the room. You feel completely accepted, and you know that this person knows you incredibly well. Like your inner critic, maybe this person has always known you as well.

Because this mystery person is so kind and loving, they sit next to your inner critic and lovingly put their hand on her arm. The inner critic seems to melt from the touch. Their eyes meet for just a moment, and then the inner critic smiles, and seems to relax a little. Next, the mystery person turns toward you, and somehow seems to know precisely what you need in this moment. You simply stand there and, like magic, you hear their words in your ears—the words that you so want to hear, so need to hear, and probably have needed to hear for a long time.

Maybe the words are "You are loved" or "You are perfect just the way you are!" or "Don't worry, everything is going to be okay." Regardless, the words you hear are the best gift you've ever received, because they make you feel totally at peace with yourself and with how you are living your life right now.

When you're ready, you say good-bye to your guests in any way you'd like. You smile as they walk out, knowing you can call them back whenever you want. You might even want to call upon the inner critic, who, although weakened, is still strong enough to guide you when you step out of line. Or you might want to call upon the mystery being when you need a little love or a few words of support…which we all need from time to time.

You relax in a chair, looking around the room filled with all your favorite things, thinking about your encounter with the inner critic and the mystery being…and then it comes to you—the mystery being is your own true voice! They looked familiar because they looked and felt like you, but different somehow, more content, more at ease. They are the voice inside you that loves you completely, that is there to help you, to support you, to tell you the loving words you need to hear. The voice of self-kindness. It had been covered up by so many other voices that you didn't hear it very much.

But now you realize that all you have to do is go back to that room in your mind, where you feel safe, and let in your own true voice. You can name her too.

Practicing with the Words of Our Own True Voice

We all have this kind voice inside that loves us. But most of us have been giving our inner critic the run of the place for so long, we often have trouble hearing our own true voice. So we need to practice.

One practice is something called loving-kindness practice, or in the original Pali language, *metta* practice. Research conducted by Barbara Fredrickson and her colleagues at the University of North Carolina found that loving-kindness practice promotes positive emotions, like happiness, which then produces less depression and more satisfaction with your life. Also, the more you practice, the better you feel (Fredrickson, 2008; Fredrickson et al, 2017).

This is a guided formal meditation, which means that it's good to set aside five or ten minutes a day to do it. This helps to develop a habit, and once it's a habit, it's a lot easier to remember to do it.

Meditation: Kindness for Someone You Care About

You can download audio for this meditation at http://www.newharbinger.com/45274.

- Find a comfortable position and take a few deep breaths, letting your body relax and your eyes close (if it's comfortable for you).

- Now bring to mind the image of someone who makes you smile when you think of them—someone you have an easy relationship with. This could be a grandparent, a friend, or even your dog or cat. You'll be repeating some kind wishes for this other being. They might be the words that your own true voice said to you, or perhaps there are other words. Here are some wishes you can try:.

  - I wish for you to feel loved.

  - I wish for you to feel happy.

  - I wish for you to feel safe and protected.

- Take a few minutes to repeat these phrases to yourself for this other person—either aloud or silently in your mind. As you do, think about the meaning behind the words.

- Next, bring in an image of yourself with this being that makes you smile. This time, repeat the phrases for both of you. You can choose different phrases, or the same ones as last time.

  - I wish for both of us to feel loved.

  - I wish for both of us to feel happy.

  - I wish for both of us to feel safe and protected.

- Now, let go of the image of the other person, so that just your own image remains in your mind. Again, repeat these phrases slowly, so that they're not simply words, but the meaning that resonates behind them:

  - I wish to feel loved.

  - I wish to feel happy.

  - I wish to feel safe and protected.

- Silently repeat those phrases again and again, using whatever words or phrases resonate most for you. Try to do this for at least five minutes. When your mind wanders, which it will because that's what minds do, just simply notice that—without judging yourself for it—and simply come back to repeating the words.

Finding Your Own Phrases

The words "loved," "happy," and "safe and protected" won't ring quite as true for some as they will for others. Feel free to experiment with trying different phrases or words. Here are a few guidelines:

- The wishes should be simple, authentic, and kind. Try not to overthink it. A good way to figure out what would work for you is to ask yourself "What do I need?" or "What do I need to hear right now?" See what your answers to these questions are, and try inserting them into the phrases.

- The words that will work best for you are the ones that, when you hear them, you say "Yep! That's just what I needed to hear!"

- It's best if these wishes are kept general. For example, it's better to say "I wish to be successful" than "I wish to get into Harvard."

- Make sure that there is not an argument in your mind when you say the phrases. For example, if you say "I wish to be happy" and a voice inside you says "Who do you think you are? You don't deserve to be happy!" it's best to modify the phrase. For example, you might want to say "I wish that one day I'll be open to being happy" or "I wish to be happy one day."

This is a formal practice, one we put aside some time to do each day. But sometimes something happens, like the situation in the cafeteria, and we need a little kindness in that moment. We may not have five minutes to do a kindness practice or even three mindful breaths to focus our wandering mind. At these times—when we need relief on the spot—we can do an informal practice.

Here's one of my favorites for you to try out. Supportive touch works because it activates a biological response in our bodies—the release of the hormone oxytocin, the "feel good" hormone. It's the hormone that's released when a mother caresses her infant's cheek, when you pet your dog or cat—the dog is content, the cat purrs, and you feel better.

Supportive Touch

You can download audio for this meditation at http://www.newharbinger.com/45274.

Because everyone differs in what they find soothing, below you'll find a variety of different ways to experience supportive touch. Find the ones that feel best to you. Try these with your eyes closed if you can, so that you can really notice the physical sensations without being distracted by the outside world. Go slowly and take a few moments with each, to really sense how each gesture feels to you.

- Put one hand over your heart. Notice the sensation of your hand on your heart.

- Put two hands on your heart. Notice how it feels, having both hands over your heart.

- Make a fist with one hand and put that hand over your heart. Maybe try putting your other hand on top of the fist.

- Put your hands in your lap and stroke one hand with the other hand. (This one is "handy" because no one has to see you doing it.)

- Fold your arms across your chest and give yourself a hug (this one can also be done without anyone noticing).

- Gently stroke one arm with the other hand.

- Cradle both cheeks with your hands.

- With your two hands, very gently tap your face all over, your forehead, your cheeks, your chin.

- Make two loose fists and gently tap your chest.

- Reach over with one hand and pat yourself on the back.

Hopefully, you found one or two gestures that feel good and make you feel a little calmer, and more centered. Next time you need on-the-go relief—you're feeling stressed or your inner critic is really hammering you—try supporting yourself with touch.

Self-Kindness Behaviors You Might Already Do

There are lots of other ways to be kind to yourself—some of these you may already be doing without knowing it. You wouldn't have survived this long if you hadn't been kind to yourself at times. Maybe when you're feeling down you do things like:

- watch a movie
- talk to a friend
- read a good book
- hang out with your dog or cat
- go for a run
- play sports
- take a nap
- take a relaxing bath
- play a video game
- put on music and dance
- text a friend

Give yourself a pat on the back when you take time to do these things. You're not being selfish—you're simply taking care of yourself. When my daughter was upset when she was little, she'd get her guinea pig out of its cage and I'd find her in her room with tears rolling down her cheeks and Oreo in her lap, stroking its fur. She didn't know it at the time, but petting Oreo released chemicals in her body that were soothing to her.

Another thing that you might already be doing to wind down is listening to music. The practice below will show how music can be helpful when you're struggling. Turning on music can be a way of turning down the volume on the inner critic.

Music Meditation

Pick a piece of music that does not have words—for this practice, it's important to use instrumental music only. Words make us start thinking, and what we really want to do is feel the music. And the music should also be soothing—as much fun as electronic music is to dance to, here something relaxing will work best.

There's only one instruction for music meditation, but it's super important: Simply pay attention to the music. Do nothing else but listen to the music. No homework, no chores, no texting, no phone, no computer...just listening..

As you listen to the music, at some point you'll probably notice that you're thinking about an upcoming party, homework, or something else. Totally normal! When this happens, just simply refocus your attention and listen to the music.

That's it! Easy, right? You didn't think listening to music could be a meditation, did you? And you can do this for as long as you'd like—five minutes, ten minutes, an hour.

Conclusion

All humans on the planet deserve to be treated with kindness. We treat our good friends with kindness, and we can treat ourselves with kindness as well. Most of us are simply out of practice. But the more we practice, the easier it becomes, and the more that nagging inner critic quiets and allows our own true voice to be heard. Being human means that we'll run into difficult moments in life, and so it's good to have some tools on hand, with which we can be kind to ourselves when those moments come up. In the next chapter, we're going to talk about other ways—really simple ways—that can help us find moments of pure joy, mixed among the difficult moments.

CHAPTER 4

Finding Wonder in the Little Things

Sometimes it's hard to notice the little things that make us happy. The hard stuff is there every day, right in front of our noses—our screw-ups on tests, the dumb thing we said to the person we like, or the bad pass on the soccer field. We're highly aware of the upsetting things that happen all day long.

But somehow, we often miss seeing the joy, or the wonder in everyday things. Why is that? Well, you may think it's because there isn't anything joyful in your life—but I am here to tell you, even without knowing your life, that you are wrong. No matter how difficult your current circumstances may be, (and I'm sure some of you are dealing with very challenging situations) there is always something joyful to be found. Something that makes you wonder. Wonder and joy are everywhere. You just need to get into the habit of looking.

Wonder and Negativity Bias

You may be asking yourself, *What does she mean by "wonder?"* I'm referring to the things in our lives, sometimes little and sometimes big, that have the potential to bring us joy. That bring a lightness to our hearts. That, even for just a moment, make us smile. Occasionally we notice them, but most of the time we don't.

Why is it that we tend to see all the crappy things in our lives but somehow miss all the good things? That seems so unfair! Well, it's because of what's called "negativity bias." The phrase refers to how we're biologically wired to notice the bad stuff in our lives and not the good stuff. It's not our fault, and we're not doing anything wrong.

Evolution can explain this. Long ago, when we were out in the wilderness hunting and gathering, we had to keep watch for all the things that could harm us, such as predatory animals. We had to stay aware of where they were and what they were doing, so that we could protect ourselves from them if they attacked. Keeping an eye out for the things that could hurt us kept us alive and allowed our species to survive. If, instead, we had lounged around appreciating the things of beauty all around us—like flowers blooming and sunsets on the savanna—we probably would have gotten eaten by a wild boar or some other predator lurking around.

Today, we carry that biology with us—it's still a part of who we are. We still much more easily notice the things that have the potential to hurt us, rather than the things that bring us joy. As the psychologist and researcher Barbara Fredrickson says, "The negative screams at you, but the positive only whispers." So, how can we make a shift so that we notice the positive things more—the things that bring us joy?

First, we make it a point to develop a practice of noticing the good that we have in our lives. And once you start, you'll see that it isn't that hard, because there are good things around us all the time.

How to Find Wonder

- *Robert's Story*

  Robert lives in the inner city, in a four-story walk-up. That means that he walks up four flights of stairs to get to the small apartment where he lives with his grandmother and younger sister. The building is old—the apartment could use some new paint and the furnishings haven't been replaced in ages. Robert takes care of his little sister after school while his grandmother works at a local convenience store.

  Robert is mostly an okay student, but has ADHD, which causes a lot of challenges. Lately, he has become pretty discouraged at school. Some of his fellow students get annoyed with him when he absentmindedly drums on his desk with his pen or blurts out an answer for the fourth time—without raising his hand.

But Robert never gets too down about his challenges, because he's made it a habit to notice the things around him that make him feel better.

When he sits at the kitchen table with his little sister after school and helps her with her homework, he notices a couple of things: when it's hot out, the window is open, and he can feel a cool breeze coming through. Because the apartment is warm, the breeze feels great on his skin. Also, Robert can hear little kids playing at the playground next to his building, and their laughter carries up to his apartment— he knows that they're having a blast, and it makes him smile to hear this. And when his little sister looks up at him like he's a god or something—like he's this brilliant guy who has all the answers—that also makes him feel good.

When he starts to cook dinner for himself and his sister, the smell of the burgers frying in the pan is heavenly. Robert is reminded that he's lucky he has something to eat, because the guy on the corner asking for money certainly doesn't seem to have any food, and he knows that there are quite a few kids at his school who don't always have enough food at home.

Sure, if Robert wanted to, he could get bummed out about the fact that kids get annoyed with him, even though he can't control his blurting out in class. And sometimes he does feel upset about that. But when he makes a point of noticing the good things all around him, he feels really good, and it brings him joy.

So, wherever you are, whoever you are, there is always something around you that can bring you a moment of happiness. It may take some time to get into the practice of looking for these things, but I promise that once you get into the habit, you'll be amazed at what you find.

Here are some suggestions around how to develop the habit.

Exercise: Wonder Practice

Step 1: Be mindful. Notice things all around you, particularly physical sensations—the way the light is falling on something in the room, the feeling of your bare feet against the soft carpet. It doesn't have to be some big huge life-changing moment—in fact, it's better if it isn't.

Step 2: Now spend a little time with it. Enjoy it. Really feel the physical sensation, really allow yourself to soak it up. If your mind starts to produce thoughts, which it often does (remember, that's your mind's job), just notice them and then simply let them drift away. If you just watch your thoughts like you're standing outside them, without getting caught up in them, they will drift away. Then come back to enjoying this nice thing that's here in your life right now. Let it wash over you. Take as much time as you would like—maybe five minutes. Maybe more.

Step 3: Now see if there's something else in your surroundings right now that is enjoyable. Maybe it's some memento from your childhood that's sitting on a shelf. Notice how it's sitting there, still, minding its own business. Maybe notice the feelings that it brings up for you—memories of something that you enjoyed doing as a kid, perhaps. Let yourself feel those feelings, opening up to them. Let them be there. Allow yourself to soak up that enjoyable memory. Do this for as long as you'd like.

Step 4: Next, you can move on to something else in the room. Or if this is enough for you, you can stop here. Either way, make a habit to notice the little things in your life that really feel enjoyable, and make you smile.

Sometimes it can be a bit hard to get into the habit of noticing the wonder all around us when we have such a strong habit of noticing all the negative stuff. The Wonder Practice above was inspired by "Sense and Savor Walk," which is one of my favorite practices from the adult program *Mindful Self-Compassion*. Taking a Sense and Savor Walk offers another great way to help get you into the habit of noticing the positive stuff.

Exercise: Sense and Savor Walk

It's ideal if you can do this activity in a natural setting—in the woods, a park, or a field. Even a residential neighborhood with houses, driveways, and streets will work. But it can also work on the sidewalk in a city. Remember, wonder is everywhere.

First, find something that draws you in, like a leaf, a rock, ants on an anthill, or even a blade of grass emerging from a crack in the sidewalk. Spend time with this thing, using all your senses to take it in and enjoy it. Go slowly.

When you feel like you're ready to move on, continue walking, keeping an eye out for the next thing that draws you in. Then spend some time with that next thing. Continue doing this for as long as you'd like. Notice how you feel at the end of your walk.

Here's another variation on the Sense and Savor Walk that's super easy and fun to do.

Exercise: Photographing Wonder

For this practice, you will take notice of things that make you smile—things that bring you joy—and take photos of them with your phone. You can take as many photos as you want, and then save them to a special folder on your phone or on your computer—it doesn't matter where, as long as you can access them easily. Then, when you're feeling down, you can simply go to this folder and look at the photos, and you'll notice a shift in how you feel.

For an added bonus, you might want to try doing this practice with a couple friends. Then you can share your photos with each other, and watch what happens! You'll be amazed at how much joy you'll bring one another. There are certain things that we all share as humans—

some of these are our emotional struggles—and that's what common humanity is all about. But some of it is also the joy that we experience when we connect with others. Sharing things that we find interesting or bring us joy can help us do just that.

Here's yet another variation of this practice.

Exercise: #MomentofJoy

As you go through your day, notice things that bring you a moment of joy or wonder. Again, remember that it can be something super small and seemingly insignificant—like the taste of a warm cup of hot chocolate or tea after being outside in the cold, or the feeling of a soft blanket that you wrap around yourself as you watch TV.

Take a photo of this thing, and share it on social media, with a comment about how or why it brought you joy, and with the hashtag #Moment ofJoy. Over time, you'll build a collection of your own moments of joy, that you can go back to whenever you'd like—and experience those moments of joy again, through your memory of them. You'll also know that you're sharing these moments with others, and that others might also get some enjoyment from them too.

The following practice has been recommended by a number of psychologists and researchers, most notably Bryan Sexton and Kathryn Adair, both from Duke University, and research has shown that doing it consistently brings greater happiness. It's yet another way to focus on the things that bring us joy—and it's super simple (Sexton and Adair, 2019).

Exercise: Three Good Things

Step 1: At the end of the day, write down three things that went well for you that day, and reflect on why they went well, and in particular, what your part was in making them happen.

Step 2: What emotion best fits how you feel about each good thing? Examples of emotions that you might be feeling are joy, gratitude, hope, excitement. Jot it down too.

Step 3: Do this every day for at least a week. Two weeks is even better.

That's it! Super simple, right? If you go to YouTube and search under "Three Good Things," you'll find lots of talks about it. And if you search your app store for "Three Good Things," you'll find apps that you can use to do the practice.

The important thing to remember with all these practices is that they don't have to be big things, like winning an award. They can be something small and simple, like an enjoyable talk with a friend at lunch, or a funny snapchat from your goofy sister. These kinds of things happen all day long—we simply have to make the habit of noticing them.

Habits take time to develop, so don't be disheartened—or criticize yourself—when you forget to notice the joy in your life, and get caught in negativity bias. You are human, after all, and you can always start again. I promise, if you keep reminding yourself, you will eventually develop the habit, and then before you know it you'll be doing it without realizing it—you'll notice that it's become super easy, and maybe even fun!

Alice Herz-Sommer, a Holocaust survivor and concert pianist who lived to be 110, attributes her long life to always looking toward the good, saying "There is beauty everywhere. I know about the bad things, but I look to the good things." You can Google her—there are several interviews with her on YouTube.

The positive outcomes that we get out of looking toward the good have been documented by a number of researchers, but most notably by Barbara Fredrickson. Fredrickson developed what's called the Broaden and Build theory, which explains that when we notice the good in our lives, we experience positive emotions, which actually broadens our awareness and perspective and helps us build personal resources, such as resilience. Experiencing positive emotions, such as joy and contentment, also allows us to become more creative and playful, and to take greater interest in exploring new things, for example. This then leads us to having new strengths and resources that provide support to us, like developing and maintaining friendships, stimulating brain development, all of which helps us to flourish.

In other words, by noticing and making room for the positive things in our lives, we feel happier, and are then able to open up to more varied experiences in our lives, leading to building our resources and our capability to handle challenges. This ultimately allows us to have greater overall well-being, and the ability to bounce back more easily when something does hurt us (Fredrickson, 2001).

Meditation: Finding Wonder in an Unexpected Place

You can download audio for this meditation at http://www.newharbinger.com/45274.

We've talked a lot about finding wonder all around us in our daily lives. Now we're going to do a guided meditation to help us find wonder in another place—somewhere you'd least expect it. This meditation was inspired by my friend Blair Carleton, a super-awesome self-compassion teacher, as well as by a practice from the Mindful Self-Compassion program.

- Find a comfortable place to sit or lie down. If you're comfortable closing your eyes, you can close them, but if not just keep a soft gaze on the floor in front of you.

- Notice any sensations in your body, including any tension, like maybe in your neck or shoulders. If you find places in your body that feel tense or even painful, bring a softening to these areas. See if you can imagine bringing some warmth, like a warm washcloth, to these areas, and see if this helps them to relax a little. Spend as much time as you need with this step.

- Take three relaxing breaths, noticing the feeling of your breath as you breathe in and as you breathe out. Try to make your out-breath a little longer than your in-breath, which engages the part of your nervous system that is responsible for relaxing. With each out-breath, allow your body to settle a little more, allowing it to let go a little more and sink a little deeper into the chair or couch.

- Let the couch, chair, or floor hold you and support you. Know that you are safe here and your body is supported.

- Now bring your attention to a faraway sound. Turn toward the sound, open to it, allow it to fill your ears. Really pay attention to it. It helps if you choose a sound that's pleasing to you, but it doesn't have to be—it can be any sound.

- Stay with the sound for a few moments. If you notice your mind wandering, gently guide your attention back to the sound.

- When you're ready, shift your attention to a sound that's closer, perhaps even in the same room as you. Pay attention to the sound, turning toward it. Allow this sound to fill your ears. Imagine that nothing else exists but this sound. Again, it's helpful if it's enjoyable, but it doesn't have to be.

- Stay with this sound for several minutes—and again, when your mind wanders, gently guide your attention back to the sound.

- Now shift your attention even closer in, to a sensation on the surface of your skin: a place where your body is in contact with the chair you're sitting in, or the sensation of your lips as they press against each other, or how your clothing feels against your skin. It's ideal if this is a sensation that is comforting, like the cushiony feeling of the couch as your body sinks into it.

- Notice the sensation and bring your attention to this place. Enjoy the sensation, feeling grateful for it. Appreciate this moment of ease. Stay with this feeling for several minutes.

- After several minutes, come closer in yet, and notice a feeling you have inside you—something deep within you, an integral part of who you are. It doesn't have to be a big deal, it can be something really small—but it should be something real, something that deep down, you truly like about yourself. Maybe it's your passion for animals, or that you're a loyal friend or that you love playing soccer so you work really hard at it. Just see what's there, some quality that you're truly glad you have, even if you don't act on it all the time. It can just be your intention to be kind. No one is listening to your thoughts, so you can be honest with yourself.

- Allow yourself to really hear that thing that you appreciate about yourself. Let it be loud and clear in your mind. Let it fill your being.

- Perhaps, as you think about this quality, you notice that you have this quality in part because of others' influence—parents, grandparents, teachers, friends, or even books you've read or maybe movies you've seen. Allow yourself to appreciate those influences in your life, maybe mentally saying a word of thanks to them. Appreciating them for this gift they have helped support in you.

- Finally, most importantly, take a moment to appreciate yourself for having this quality. Remember that little things can fill us with wonder too. All we have to do is pay attention to them.

- When you are ready, gently open your eyes.

Take a moment to reflect on how this practice was for you. Perhaps it was pretty straightforward and easy. For some people, however, it can be pretty challenging—if that's you, know that you are not alone, and it will become easier with practice. We aren't used to appreciating the good qualities about ourselves. Most of us have no problem appreciating the good qualities of others, but paying attention to our own might make us feel guilty or selfish.

Trust me, there's nothing wrong with loving and appreciating yourself. In fact, that's what this whole book is all about—understanding how treating yourself with kindness helps you to stress less and be less hard on yourself. And it makes you feel more confident, so you can be a better friend to others since you have more to give. You're building your strength and resilience so that you can be there not just for yourself, but for others also.

Conclusion

Wonder and the potential for joy are everywhere, outside of you and inside of you, and if you take the time to simply pause, to notice and bring awareness to these things in your life, you end up feeling happier. Bringing awareness to moments of wonder in our lives is part of mindfulness. Noticing that they are part of the human experience—that's part of common humanity. As human beings, we all have the capacity to experience wonder and joy. Fully immersing ourselves in a feeling of joy is an act of self-kindness in itself.

Wonder brings together all three components of self-compassion: mindfulness, common humanity, and self-kindness. And the funny thing is, when you are noticing the wonder around you, your problems seem to fade into the background. You're not so focused on yourself, and as a result you are less hung up on any negativity or self-criticism going on in your mind.

In the next section, we're going to take all of the self-compassion skills you've learned in the first part of the book and apply them to dealing with the kinds of struggles that you encounter every day—school stress, challenges with social media, dealing with relationships and body issues, and for some teens, facing gender and sexuality issues. Self-compassion is all about giving ourselves tools to help deal with the kinds of challenges we run into in our daily lives, and the self-criticism that often emerges when being faced by them.

CHAPTER 5

School Stress—It Doesn't Have to Defeat You

Let's say you have a big history group project due on Friday. The group that you chose to work with isn't exactly working, to put it mildly. They all seem to have better things to do—at least, better for them. You, on the other hand, want to get a decent grade on this project. You have an A in the class so far, and this project is worth a lot of your grade. But your teammates aren't acting like a team, and you are growing more and more frustrated, and angry at yourself. You should have known better. You should have known when these popular kids agreed to work with you that you'd get stuck doing the whole thing yourself.

You feel like an idiot. You're going to end up getting a bad grade just because you wanted to work with the popular kids. On top of that, you have a huge math exam tomorrow that covers everything you've learned this quarter, and you can't focus on studying—you're so distracted thinking about this stupid history project, and your stupid decision to work with these kids, rather than the smart kids who would actually be doing their share of the project.

Pressure from Others

School stress—sometimes it feels overwhelming. In addition to the actual pile-up of all the assignments, you have your parents telling you constantly how important it is to get good grades so that you can get into a good college. According to them, if you don't get into a good college you're doomed for life.

And then your teachers are telling you how important your grades are because they are on your record forever. You don't even know what that means, but it sounds terrifying. And the school counselor is telling you that you aren't working up to your potential—whatever that means. How do they even know what your potential is?

Sometimes it feels like the pressure is unbearable. And you just want to scream—or retreat into a corner of your room and binge-watch *Stranger Things*. Every single episode.

What can you do to reduce this stress? First, know that you are not alone. According to the American Psychological Association, 83 percent of teens say that school is a significant source of stress (APA, 2014).

Second, know that this is not your fault. Our twenty-first-century schools put tremendous pressure on kids to perform. The number of AP classes offered at many schools has increased dramatically in the last thirty years, and schools encourage students to take them because, in part, it makes the school look better if students are taking higher-level classes. High school students often get homework over summer break; not that long ago, summer meant you actually had a break from schoolwork, time to rest and relax. On top of all of that, getting into college has become increasingly more competitive. And unfortunately, some people judge you not on things that might really matter, like what kind of person you are, whether you are generous or kind or a good friend, for example, but on external factors like your grades, your rank in your graduating class, or what college you're going to.

The result of society's pressure on teens is that teens report high levels of stress. The American Psychological Association surveyed teens and reported in 2014 that 27 percent of teens report a stress level during the school year of eight, nine, or ten on a 10-point scale. Moreover, 31 percent of teens said that their stress level had increased in the last year, and 34 percent expected their stress level to increase in the coming year.

Doing Your Best and Still Not Measuring Up

You may put pressure on yourself to become the successful person that all the adults in your life want you to be. And yet maybe there's this little voice inside you crying out, "This is too much for me! Maybe I'm just not smart enough! Maybe I don't have what it takes! Why can't I relax and just be me! Why can't that be enough?"

How can you be yourself amid all this pressure to be the perfect honor roll student or all-state athlete that everyone wants you to be? Maybe you feel like a total failure because you simply can't seem to measure up, can't seem to sail through your schoolwork and be that A student that everyone thinks somehow you should be. What can you do?

Here's one idea: In the middle of all this stress-making craziness, you can be a good friend to yourself. You can be a support to yourself. You can be there for yourself to calm yourself down, to tell yourself it will all be okay, that it will all work out one way or another. In other words, tell yourself precisely what you would tell a good friend who was going through the same thing. If you can say it to a good friend, you can say it to yourself, right? And, if you're not so sure that it matters whether you're a good friend to yourself, think of it this way: Research tells us that when we are kinder to ourselves, we are less stressed, less depressed, and less anxious. And of course, being less stressed helps you do better in school. So, being kind to yourself can actually, in the long run, reduce school-related stress and help you be more effective.

The next practice will show you how you can do this. It's called Compassionate Friend, and the original version comes from Paul Gilbert, founder of compassion-focused therapy (CFT); this version is from the teen self-compassion program Making Friends with Yourself. An important thing to remember when you're doing this practice, and actually all practices in this book, is to do them slowly. There's no rush—this isn't school, and it's actually not more efficient or effective to get done quickly. It's important to allow the words to sink in, and to do that you have to take your time and proceed slowly. It will work its magic better that way.

Meditation: Compassionate Friend

You can download audio for this meditation at http://www.newharbinger.com/45274.

- Either seated or lying down, close your eyes and take a few deep breaths. Allow yourself to relax, and let the chair or ground support you. With each breath, see if you can let go a little more, and relax a little more.

- Now allow yourself to imagine a place where you feel safe, comfortable, and relaxed—this can be a real place or an imagined place, but it should be a place that allows you to breathe comfortably and let go of any worry. Perhaps in nature—a beach, a place in the woods near a brook—or maybe it's a corner of your bedroom or the comfort of a good friend's house. It might even be an imaginary place, like floating on a cloud, or maybe a room full of super-comfy quilts. Imagine this place in as much detail as you can—the sounds, the smells, any physical sensations, and most of all what you feel like in this place.

- Soon you'll receive a visitor…a warm and kind friend. This is someone who loves you completely and accepts you exactly for who you are. This can be real person—a friend, maybe a grandparent, or a favorite teacher—or it can be someone from a book you've read, a pet, a superhero, or even a character from a comic book or movie. Or it can be some being that you create in your mind. Imagine this being in as much detail as possible, especially how it feels to be in their presence.

- Soon you will be greeting your kind friend. You have a choice— you can either go out from your safe place to meet your friend or you can invite them in. Either way is fine; do whichever is most comfortable for you. Imagine that you are doing that now.

- Now imagine yourself sitting with the person at just the right distance away from them—whatever feels right for you. You feel completely comfortable and safe, completely accepted and loved. This is just where you need to be right now.

- Take a moment to enjoy how you feel in the presence of your special friend. This being is here with you now and understands exactly what it's like to be you, exactly where you are in your life right now, and precisely what you struggle with. This being knows that you are doing the best you can for where you are in your life. They know you better than anyone else, and they love and accept you completely. Even when you fail—especially when you fail.

- This being has something important to say to you, something that's *exactly what you need to hear right now.* See if you can listen closely for the words they want to share, words that are comforting, supportive, and kind. Maybe something like "Don't be so hard on yourself for choosing those kids to do the history project with. You just want to be accepted and loved. That is totally human. We all want to be loved." And if no words come, that's okay too. Just enjoy being in the presence of your compassionate friend.

- Now, maybe you have something you'd like to say to your friend. This friend is a very good listener, and completely understands you. Is there anything you'd like to say?

- Enjoy your friend's good company for a few last moments, and wave good-bye to them, knowing you can invite them back whenever you need to.

- You are now alone in your safe place again. Spend a few moments thinking about what just happened, maybe reflecting on the words you heard.

- And before this meditation ends, please remember that this compassionate friend is a *part of you.* The loving presence you felt and the words you heard are a deep part of yourself. The comfort and safety that you may be feeling is there within you at all times. Know that you can return to this safe place and to this compassionate friend whenever you need to.

- Now bring your attention back to your breath, and when you feel ready, gently open your eyes.

Were you surprised to find that the kind friend was actually a part of you? When most people—both adults and teens—finish this meditation, they are often surprised that the friend is actually a voice inside them. But it has to be, right? Because you created this being in your mind. You thought up what they looked like, how you felt in their presence, the words they said. So truly, this means that you have this kind, loving voice inside you at all times—this kind voice that will offer you support and acceptance whenever you need it. Your own true voice.

Fear of Failing

So, if this kind, loving voice is always within us, why don't we usually hear it? In contrast, we have this loud, obnoxious, critical voice that is shouting at us all the time, telling us that we aren't trying hard enough, that we can do better. And part of us undoubtedly listens to this voice, believing that if we only worked harder, we'd achieve more. We'd get that good grade, or the part in the school play, or first chair in the orchestra, or make the team.

We listen to this voice because it's a habit—we've been doing it our whole lives. We have the habit of being hard on ourselves for lots of reasons, and one of them is because we think we will achieve more if we're hard on ourselves. We're afraid that if we are kind to ourselves, we'll end up like a blob on the couch, stuffing our faces with Doritos and binging on Netflix.

Interestingly, research tells us the opposite. Research tells us that when we are kinder to ourselves, we are more likely to try new things and achieve more. We aren't so afraid of failing.

You might be thinking, *Wait, what*? *Afraid of failing*? *Explain this please.*

At times, people are often reluctant to try new things, because they're afraid they'll fail at them. They'd rather play it safe and do something they know how to do well than stick their neck out and try something new. If you've ever felt like that, know that many people feel that way at times, and it's quite natural.

Sometimes, people get to a point where they give up, and aren't trying anymore.

• *Dave's Story*

Take Dave, for example. Although Dave loved to learn, and was really smart, his disability made it really hard for him to learn to read. In early elementary school he did

79

great—until reading became really important and necessary for all the other subjects. By fourth and fifth grade, he had to read well to do well in science, history, English, and even math. It was just too hard for him, he couldn't keep up, and no one recognized that he had a disability. By the time he got to high school he had given up on school, and just wasn't trying anymore. He figured even if he did, he'd fail anyway, so why bother? The really sad thing was, he was awesome at math, but because he never tried, no one— including him—ever got to see how smart he was.

If you never really try, there's still a possibility that if you did try you would succeed. If you do try, though, that means you risk failing. Because of this risk, some people figure that it's better to play it safe and not know if they would succeed, rather than trying their best and possibly failing anyway.

You may be thinking that this sounds like you. Maybe you aren't doing your best at school right now. Maybe you're afraid of failing, and that's why you spend so much time playing video games when you should be doing your homework. Failing is hard enough on its own, but failing even though you tried your best can be a lot harder—and scarier.

• *Demetrius's Story*

Demetrius had a choice between taking a regular English class or one that was a little more challenging. English had always been his best subject, and his parents thought he should take the challenging class. But Demetrius knew that if he took the challenging one and didn't do well, he would feel really embarrassed, because he'd always thought of himself as a good writer. In fact, he'd always been one of the best English students in his class—people sometimes call him "Shakespeare" because his grades are so high. Demetrius liked the positive attention he got for standing out in English class, so he thought that maybe he should play it safe and stick with the regular class, where he knows he can succeed. He didn't want to take the chance of not standing out in the hard class—or, who knows, maybe even failing.

All of us have a fear of failure, to some degree. It comes from wanting to be accepted by others, to belong, to be part of a group. There's nothing wrong with this—it's part of who we are as humans. Needing to belong is a basic need that we all have. It helps us to feel accepted, loved, and connected to others.

But what can we do about fear of failure when it interferes with our ability to do our best? How can we take on challenges without the fear of failing—or maybe just a little less fear of failing? And what does being kind to ourselves have to do with this anyway?

You guessed it—self-compassion. Research has shown that when people are kinder to themselves, they have less fear of failure, and are more able to take on challenges. Like hard English classes, or trying a new sport, or a new musical instrument.

Let's try a new self-compassion practice. This one is usually done as a formal practice, one that you set aside ten minutes or so to do, but you can also do it quickly, in the moment when you're feeling stressed, as an informal practice.

Earlier you discovered kindness phrases that were tailor-made for you. Now we're going to use those phrases in this kindness practice—to help us to develop the practice of being kind to ourselves. And remember: As my co-teacher and friend Laura Prochnow Phillips likes to say, "It's not like pie. You don't have a finite amount of kindness to give." In other words, just because you are giving yourself kindness, that doesn't mean that you have less to give to others. In fact, giving yourself kindness allows you to fill yourself up, so that you actually have more to give to others. It's an interesting thing about self-compassion—the more you give yourself, the more you have to give others.

Kindness for Me

You can download audio for this meditation at
http://www.newharbinger.com/45274.

- Recall the words or phrases that you came up with when you did the exercise "Finding Your Own Phrases." You might also want to take a look at those phrases, to review them if you need to. Call those phrases to mind now.

- Try to relax when doing this practice, and not to worry so much if you're doing it right—just let the words do the work, kind of like slipping into a bath and letting the warm water relax you.

- Now find a comfortable position, sitting or lying down, and let your eyes close, fully or partially. Take a few deep breaths, to settle into your body, allowing your body to sink a little deeper into the chair or couch each time you breathe out.

- Put your hand over your heart, or wherever feels comforting and supportive, as a reminder that this whole practice is about being kind to yourself in this very moment.

- Feel your breath move in your body, wherever you notice it most easily. Feel the gentle rhythm of your breathing, one breath at a time. When your attention wanders, no need to judge your-self—simply come back to noticing the gentle movement of your breath.

- After a few minutes of paying attention to your breath, let go of the focus on your breathing, and begin to say to yourself the words or phrases that you came up with, that are most meaning-ful to you. Imagine that you are whispering them into your own ear. You have nothing to do, and nowhere to go—no homework, no chores. Your only job right now is to simply listen to these kind words, letting them wash over you and through you, letting them fill your being.

- Whenever you notice that your mind has wandered, simply come back to these words. Always returning to the words, again and again. Like the phrases are your home base, and you're coming home to them, over and over.

- Take a few more minutes to silently repeat these words or phrases to yourself. And when you're ready to move on, let go of the phrases and take a minute or two to rest quietly in your own body. Then slowly open your eyes.

This kindness practice can be quite subtle. Often we don't notice anything different for some time after doing it—even if we're doing it every day. Then one day, we may notice that we're not as hard on ourselves as we have been previously. Sharon Salzberg, a renowned meditation teacher, tells the story of what happened to her when she first began doing kindness practice. She was on a retreat—a place where you go to do these practices intensively for a week or two. She was doing loving-kindness practice intensively. After about a week she didn't notice any difference, and was a bit dismayed. She then accidentally knocked over a glass vase in her room, and noticed that the words she immediately said to herself were "What a klutz! But I love you anyway!" She related that she was sure that she wouldn't have added the "But I love you anyway" had she not been doing kindness practice all week.

Another story comes from the Jewish tradition. A student asked a rabbi why it says in the Torah, the Jewish holy book, that we put the holy words—the words of kindness—"upon" our hearts, rather than "in" our hearts. The rabbi responded that our hearts are often closed, because we have struggled and been hurt in our lives. Our hearts are tight with suffering. Yet one day our hearts will break open, and the kind words will fall in.

So we do these kindness practices for ourselves, not to change who we are, but simply to put them on our hearts, knowing that one day our hearts will soften and we will really hear these words, take them in, deep into our core. One day they will become an integral part of who we are, and we will truly believe them. And when we do, the way we see ourselves will have changed—we won't be so afraid of failing, and we will be more easily able to take on a challenge without feeling stressed.

You may be thinking, *But I'm applying to college in a year or two, and I'm stressed about my grades. I can't wait for the words to sink in! I'm freaking out now!*

For right now, we can offer you another practice. This one is mostly a mindfulness practice and is super-helpful for reducing anxiety.

Exercise: Everything in the Palm of Your Hand

You can download audio for this exercise at
http://www.newharbinger.com/45274.

This is an informal practice that brings you to the present moment easily and quickly.

- Open the palm of your hand. Take a good look at it, noticing the slightly different shades of skin on your palm. Look closely at the lines—notice how the creases might lead into each other, or there might be little creases coming out of the bigger, main creases. Notice the difference in coloration between the main creases, the little creases, and the rest of the palm of your hand.

- Experiment with stretching your hand out so that your fingers bend back slightly and the skin is stretched taut across your hand. Do you notice any changes in the lines on your hand? How does it feel when you stretch your hand out like this? What sensations do you notice? What happens when you stretch it out even further? What do you notice now? What about if you hold that stretch for a minute or more? Do you notice any thoughts coming up in your mind?

- Now relax your hand and let the fingers naturally curl slightly inward. How does this change the sensations that you can feel, and what the palm of your hand looks like? Relax your hand even more, and see what happens to your fingers and your palm. Any changes in the color or the creases in your hand? Any changes in your thoughts?

- Now, with one finger of your other hand, gently trace the lines in your palm. Notice the physical sensation. Keep your attention on the point of contact, where your finger touches the palm of your hand. What does it feel like?

- Next, close your eyes and make slow circles with your finger around the surface of your palm, keeping your attention on the sensations. When your mind wanders, gently guide your attention back to the sensation of your finger on your palm. Notice what the sensation is like when you trace your palm to the tips of each finger.

- You can do this for as long as you like. When you're ready, gently open your eyes.

As you were doing this practice, you may have noticed that you weren't worrying and stressing so much. That's because you were staying in the present moment by using your senses—your sense of sight and your sense of touch. As we've learned, physical sensations keep you in the present moment, and allow you to let go of the past and future, where worry and stress take place.

The nice thing about this practice is that you can do it anywhere—on the school bus, waiting in a doctor's office, or sitting in a class waiting for an exam to begin. You can simply surreptitiously pay attention to the palm of your hand—in a way that no one will notice. As long as you continue to guide your attention back to the lines in your hand, or the sensations as you trace the lines, your mind will let go of the story that you're stressed about—the test you're about to take, for example—and you'll feel less anxious.

Conclusion

Stress about school has skyrocketed. Much of it can be attributed to pressures from society and schools themselves. One way to deal with this stress is to be a kind friend to yourself, not putting more pressure on yourself; knowing that you will stay motivated without the additional push. And, don't forget, research has shown that treating yourself with kindness can actually decrease your depression, anxiety, and stress, which will help you get your schoolwork done well—which in turn will help you reduce your stress load even more.

Research also tells us that when we are kinder to ourselves, we are more comfortable moving outside of our comfort zone to explore new things, expanding our abilities and what we know. Mindfulness practices in the moment such as "Everything in the Palm of Your Hand" can also help reduce anxiety, and internalizing the message of kind words you can say to yourself can help to reduce the fear of failure, allowing you to build resilience and to move forward with strength, integrity, and determination.

CHAPTER 6

Social Media: How to Stop Comparing Yourself to Others

You pick up your phone, check out your latest post, and see that there are only two likes. If you're like many of us, your inner critic probably takes over. *What? Does no one see me? No one seems to even notice me or what I have to say. And there it is for everyone to see, all over the Internet. Only two likes. Scroll down, and there's Letitia's post with seventy-three likes! She's obviously having a blast at some party somewhere while I'm stuck at home with two pathetic likes. I feel like I don't exist.*

Social media can make you feel this way sometimes. Don't get me wrong, there are some really great things about it—sometimes it allows you to connect with others, especially when you're feeling alone. Sometimes it might feel really good to sit in your room and chat with your friends, sharing different aspects of your lives. Social media can help you feel included and part of a group. But at other times, social media can make you feel a lot worse.

Let's try an exercise to explore how you use social media, and the effect it has on you. This exercise comes from a self-compassion program developed for young adults; this particular exercise was inspired by Alayna Fender.

Exercise: Exploring Social Media

You can download audio for this exercise at http://www.newharbinger.com/45274.

You'll need a pen and paper to do this exercise, so make sure you have that handy.

- You can begin by closing your eyes, fully or partially, and taking a moment to check in. Feel the movement of your breath as it flows in and out of the body. Notice how are you feeling right now, and write down any feelings that are present.

- Now take out your phone, and find your most used social media app, such as Instagram or Twitter. Take a minute to scroll through the app, paying particular attention to how what you're seeing makes you feel. Take a few minutes to do this, noticing whatever feelings arise.

- Write down any thoughts or feelings that come up while you're scrolling. For example:

- *I feel unworthy.*

- *I feel like I don't measure up.*

- *I feel angry or sad.*

- *I feel inspired.*

- *I feel like I'm not good enough.*

- *I feel entertained.*

- *I feel lonely.*

- Now gently close your eyes, and place a hand over your heart, or anywhere that feels soothing to you. Offer yourself compassion for any feelings of distress or unworthiness that may have arisen. Perhaps you can say to yourself:

  - *May I treat myself with kindness in this moment.*

  - *May I know that I am enough, just as I am.*

  - *May I begin to know my own value.*

- If you have trouble thinking of words that really sound right to you, ask yourself what you might say to a good friend who was feeling like you are in this moment. And then, if you can, say those words to yourself.

- Now ask yourself if there are any ways that you could treat yourself with more compassion when it comes to your social media usage, and write down any ideas that come up.

If you found that scrolling through social media made you feel self-critical or bad about yourself, being aware of those feelings can lead to making healthier choices around social media in the future. Offering yourself compassion for the upsetting feelings that arose can also be helpful.

"Comparison Is the Thief of Joy"— Theodore Roosevelt

What is it about social media that makes us feel bad about ourselves? We know that lots of people, both teens and adults, feel connected to others when they use social media. It's a great way to connect with friends, and even make some new ones. But as you may have noticed with this last exercise, social media also has some drawbacks, and can make us feel alone and "less than."

One of the biggest issues is that social media promotes comparison—we tend to compare our lives with others', whether in the way we look, our experiences and how we spend our time, or how popular we are. And when we compare ourselves to others, we often end up feeling pretty bad, like we don't measure up. It can feel like others are better, smarter, more attractive, and have it together so much more than we do.

We compare ourselves to others despite the fact that we know that people always post their best version of themselves—sometimes even using multiple apps and filters to make themselves look better than they really look. Of course no one posts those moments when they're feeling miserable, or hurt, or have a giant pimple in the middle of their face, or are sitting at home alone in their room with headphones on, trying to block out the world. Those moments don't make it onto social media sites.

We all have moments when we're feeling down and lonely and like we don't belong. Because we're all human. Feeling down comes with the territory of being alive and here in a human body. We all feel down sometimes. So why do we turn to our phones in those moments, knowing that it often makes us feel worse?

The Need to Belong

As humans, we have a deep need to connect with others, to feel like we belong, to be part of a group, and to be accepted. We are simply biologically wired that way, and this need to belong guides a lot of our behavior. Cliques form in school because they're a way that kids can feel like they belong. The Netflix series *13 Reasons Why* is all about our need for acceptance and connection with others. And think about fashion trends—certain fashions become trends because people want to wear what others are wearing, so that they can be part of the group. Advertising companies know that teens, in particular, are prone to wanting to belong, and they craft their advertisements to teens to appeal to their desire to fit in.

From an evolutionary perspective, the need to belong makes a lot of sense—we need our peer group, or tribe, in order to eventually find a mate and continue the species. So the primal need to belong actually makes it possible for us to find a safe place—a place where we never feel disconnected, we always feel protected, and everybody knows who we are. In other words, we are known, recognized for who we are, and this helps us to feel safe. From that standpoint, having friends and being part of a group is actually critical to our survival!

Wanting to have friends and to be part of a group is totally normal. It simply means we're human. Our friends give us support, a sense of safety, and protection.

But being on social media can threaten this sense of belonging, by pointing out all the ways that we might not be part of a group, or that others are better than us and therefore more likely to be accepted than us.

If social media is making you feel bad, how can you soothe yourself when social media triggers your inner critic, or makes you feel inadequate or lost? Let's do a practice and see if we can find out.

Exercise: What Do I Need?

You can download audio for this exercise at http://www.newharbinger.com/45274.

- Find a comfortable place to sit. Allow your shoulders to drop away from your ears, and if you're comfortable closing your eyes, allow your eyes to close. Take a few deep breaths and allow yourself to settle in. Don't rush your breathing; you need time to really relax. With each breath, allow yourself to sink a little deeper into the chair or couch.

- Now take a moment to think about this: If you could have any words whispered in your ear, and be able to hear them whenever you need to, what words would they be? You aren't going to be sharing these words with anyone—they are just for you. What words do you most want to hear?

- Maybe words like:

  - *You are safe.*

  - *You are strong.*

  - *You are accepted.*

  - *You belong.*

- Now imagine that you really hear these words—they come from your own true voice and are whispered into your ear, with a tone of warmth and unconditional love, unwavering and strong yet also gentle and kind. You hear them whispered to you again and again.

- Maybe:

  - *You will be fine.*

  - *You are perfect just as you are.*

  - *You are loved.*

  - *Everything is going to be okay.*

  - *You have everything you need.*

- Sometimes it helps to give a supportive touch while repeating these words. Perhaps you can put your hand on your heart or stroke your upper arm. Or maybe your fist is over your heart with your other hand on top of the fist.

- Take a few minutes to listen to these words. Let them sink in. Hear them again, and again. Allow yourself to absorb these kind words, these words you so need to hear.

- Now notice how you feel. You might feel a tiny bit different, or you may feel very different. However you feel is just fine.

If you feel better after doing this exercise, great. If not, you can try it again another time if you like, or you can skip it altogether. The important thing to know is that you're setting an intention to listen to your own true voice, which cares deeply about you, wants the best for you, and speaks to you from your heart. Remember that it takes some courage to listen to this voice, to pay attention to it and really hear what it has to say. And when you do feel brave enough to do this, the other voices—including the inner critic and the voices from social media—tend to fade into the background.

Stepping Away from Your Phone… If Only for a Moment

Sometimes it can be an interesting experiment to take a step away from your phone and from social media. Although we often feel we can't—or don't want to—stepping away can have interesting consequences, as Carlita found out.

- ## *Carlita's Story*

  Carlita used her phone all the time. At times, when she scrolled through her various social media platforms, like Instagram, she felt connected to friends—she saw their posts, liked them or commented on them, and others commented back. It made her feel good, accepted. Like she had a distinct and tight group of friends. Especially when these conversations were with kids she looked up to—like when popular kids at school commented on her posts.

  But then there were those other times—like the time when someone posted a photo of friends having a great time at a party that she wasn't invited to. She felt really awful about that. And then the time when her best friend—or someone she thought was her best friend—posted a photo of herself linking arms with the new girl at school, with the tag "my best friend." That made her heart sink.

But the worst was when some girl at school posted a photo of herself outside the movie theater in the arms of Carlita's crush. The crush that she'd had for two years. That was like a body blow. Carlita didn't come out of her room for an entire weekend. Her mom couldn't get through to her and was concerned about how her phone was affecting her, so took away her phone for two weeks. Carlita thought her life would end—no connection to her friends! And more, she thought she'd be bored out of her mind.

But you'll never guess what happened. Carlita found other things that she enjoyed doing, and she actually felt relieved that she didn't have to reach for her phone all the time. She discovered that she loved to draw, and her mom bought her some new art pencils and pens. And she had renewed interest in taking her dog out for walks in the woods—something she used to do with her mom when she was younger, but hadn't done in a long time.

So really, having your phone not right on you from time to time can relieve you of the burden of having to respond to all those pings and notifications. You can be alone with your thoughts, without distraction. Instead of being torn between what's going on in the moment—whether it's having dinner, talking with friends, or doing homework—and what's going on with your phone, you can simply give yourself a break, and do just one thing at a time.

Eat dinner.

Talk with friends.

Do your homework.

And guess what the research says about this? When you're doing your homework, you can focus much better if your phone is in the next room. *Even if it's turned off and sitting next to you at the table, and you never touch it,* you'll still do better on your homework if it's in the next room. Is that crazy or what? Even if it's simply sitting there on the table minding its own business, it still is distracting you so much that you'll do better if you put it where you can't see it.

Control Social Media Before It Controls You

Here are a couple of easy ways that you can exercise your control over social media so you can engage when you want to—and not have it pull you in and control you when you don't.

- Turn off notifications. This is really simple and makes a huge difference. It's simple: If notifications are on, every time you get pinged your train of thought is interrupted, and social media is in control—you get pulled into whatever story is happening, and then it takes time for you to get back into what you were doing. If you were doing something that takes a fair amount of concentration—like homework, for example—research says it takes about twenty-five minutes to re-engage! And in that time, you're likely to get pinged again, right? So you're never really able to focus completely, and it becomes much harder to do the homework at all. But, if you turn off notifications, and then get on social media when you have some free time, then you are in control—you are choosing when to engage, and you're not being led around by whatever and whenever something is posted.

- Mute accounts. On most social media sites, you can mute accounts. This is similar to unfollowing someone—except that the person doesn't know that they're not being followed. You will no longer see their posts, but they won't know that. This is helpful when someone's posts are upsetting you, but for whatever reason they might be offended if you unfollow them.

The important thing is to put yourself in charge—you have the ability to protect yourself from being interrupted, hurt, or criticized, by yourself or others. You don't have to get pulled into social media if it is hurting you in any way. It may take some courage to step back, see how social media is affecting you, and make a conscious choice to do something different, but you'll likely be glad you did.

So what should you do when social media triggers your inner critic, making you feel like you don't belong? You can try this practice. It has three parts, which you can do altogether, or one at a time.

Exercise: Working with Difficult Emotions

You can download audio for this exercise at http://www.newharbinger.com/45274.

Part 1:

Name It to Tame It

- So you've been on social media, and you notice that you're feeling upset. First, can you notice the emotion that you're feeling? Not the story, like who said what, but what you're feeling. Are you disappointed? Sad? Lonely? Anxious? Distraught? Maybe simply bored? Maybe you feel a number of different things. Be honest with yourself and see if you can identify a feeling, or more than one, then write it/them down.

- Be open to whatever you're feeling, whether positive or negative, and, using a gentle voice, simply state whatever the feeling is. (You probably want to state it silently if anyone is around or they may think you're going a bit nutty.) For example, you might be feeling lonely. If this is the case, gently say to yourself, "This is loneliness." Maybe you're feeling nervous. In that case, simply state, "This is nervousness." Kind of like you're another person, looking in from the sidelines and just noticing.

- If you'd like, you can put your hand over your heart, or another supportive touch that you find comforting, and say some kind words to yourself. You can either say them softly to yourself or silently. Maybe words like, "It's so hard feeling like I'm not included," or "It's really sad to feel unseen and unappreciated. But I know that this feeling won't last forever."

When you identify your feelings in this way, it's like you're taking a step away and creating distance between you and the feeling, so you're not being consumed by it. It also engages your prefrontal cortex, the part of your brain that is responsible for clear, logical thinking, and quiets down the amygdala, the part of your brain that gets activated when you're feeling emotional. So you feel a little less emotional, and a bit more rational.

Part 2:

Feel It to Heal It

In general, when you're feeling some kind of strong emotion, you can feel it someplace in your body. When you're feeling painful emotions, another way to give yourself a break—to be self-compassionate—is to find where the sensations related to that emotion are in your body. You can do this practice together with step 1, or you can do them separately.

- Take a moment to scan your body from head to toe, noticing any places where you might feel a little discomfort, tension, rumbling, or pulsating. Take your time to do this.

- See if you can notice a sensation, like a lump in your throat, or a heavy feeling in the bottom of your stomach, or tension in your neck. Maybe you can feel a sort of electric pulse in your heart area.

- Whatever feeling you sense, just simply allow it to be there, noticing what it feels like.

Part 3:

Softening and Opening

- Once you find the place where the emotion resides in your body, see if you can soften that area a little, maybe by imagining you're putting a warm washcloth on it, or someone is giving you a gentle massage, or you're immersing that part of your body in a warm bath.

- Now, as you breathe in, imagine that you're breathing in something soothing, something warm, and that it's going straight to this place where you feel tension or discomfort. You can feel the muscles relaxing; there is more space and more room to breathe.

- See if you can "open" to the feeling, allowing it to be there, and allowing yourself to feel the sensations of the feeling in your body.

Letting it be there. And allowing yourself to be with whatever it is that you're feeling.

- Take a moment to notice how you're feeling. Your whole body may feel a little less burdened, a little bit lighter.

It takes some courage to turn toward the feeling, to allow yourself to feel whatever is there. It takes courage because sometimes what's there doesn't feel good. It might be a sense of loneliness, or an empty feeling, or sadness. But when we turn toward it with a sense of openness and acceptance, we realize that whatever feeling is present is okay.

We can live with this difficult feeling. It's natural, it's real, and it's something that all of us as humans experience from time to time. It doesn't feel good, but by acknowledging it and allowing yourself to feel it, you may notice that it will quietly go away on its own.

Exercise: A Moment for Me

**You can download audio for this exercise at
http://www.newharbinger.com/45274.**

Here's another practice you can use when someone or something on social media makes you feel badly about yourself. You can take a moment for yourself.

- First, acknowledge whatever you're feeling. You can say words to yourself like "I'm feeling hurt right now, like I don't belong.

This feeling sucks." This is mindfulness, the first component of self-compassion.

- Second, remember that we all feel this way at times, because we all want to feel connected and like we belong. Wanting to feel like included is part of being human, and is embedded in our biology. So maybe you can say something to yourself like "I am not alone. Feeling hurt and left out is normal. It may not feel good, but we all feel this way sometimes." This is common humanity, the second part of self-compassion.

- Third, think about what a good friend might say to you. Or you can simply be quiet and see if you can hear your own true voice—knowing that this voice will say the words you most need to hear in this moment. The voice might say something like "You are absolutely fine just the way you are. You don't have to change at all. No one is perfect." Listening to your own true voice takes some courage, because you are likely not used to saying kind things to yourself. This is self-kindness, the third part of self-compassion.

Being Kind to Yourself

Stay aware of how you feel when you're on social media. Simply take a moment to pause and be aware of how it makes you feel, and do something kind for yourself if it leaves you feeling sad, disconnected, or self-critical. And if being on social media makes you feel good, go for it!

Conclusion

Remember, an important part of being kind to yourself is being your own best advocate—standing up for yourself and being kind to yourself when something is hurting you. It means noticing what makes you feel bad, then making a conscious decision about whether or not you want to keep that thing in your life.

When it comes to social media, you have the power to choose how and when to engage with it. The tools in this chapter can help you stop comparing yourself to others, notice how social media makes you feel, and take a break from it when you need to. This human need that we have to belong and be accepted plays out in so many places in our lives, and very much so in social media.

The next chapter will address another place where the need to belong and be accepted is clear: in our relationships with others. Conflicts and misunderstandings with friends and family often cause deep pain, and self-compassion is a great resource that can support you when you run up against these tough times.

CHAPTER 7

Dealing with Difficult Relationships

Friends. Parents. Dating. Relationships in your teen years are all about change.

Think about it: At age ten, you're pretty settled in with the adults in your life and maybe a sibling or two, and they're who you spend your time with when you're not in school.

But when you move into your teen years, your peers hold that starring role, and the adults in your life fade a little into the background. They're still there, but are no longer front and center. In fact, sometimes they're downright annoying. You often feel like they just don't understand you, and sometimes they treat you like you're eight years old. They don't seem to see how much you've grown and matured in the last few years.

On the other hand, your friends are pretty cool. They *get* you. They understand the pressures you're under—the challenges of academics, the social scene, and the stress of being a teen in general. They listen to you and understand.

So why do all these changes happen during your teen years? What's going on?

There are evolutionary and biological reasons that relationships change during your teen years. When you're a kid, you need your family to take care of you and protect you. An infant can't survive on its own, and children in our society need adults to feed and clothe them, to teach them right from wrong, and to show them how to function in our society. As you get older and become a teen, there are different tasks that you have to learn—tasks that you'll need to know how to do when you're an adult, which, believe it or not, is not that far away. Your brain goes through a lot of remodeling, to get you ready for adulthood.

Changes in Your Brain

During the infant and toddler years, our brains go through a huge amount of growth—because infants and toddlers have a lot of learning and adaptation to do —and need a lot of neurons (nerve cells in the brain) and synapses (spaces between nerves, across which chemical messages get transmitted). This rapid growth slows down in childhood, though, and the process of "pruning" starts to happen: nerve pathways that aren't used die off. When it comes to these neural connections, "what you don't use, you lose." This is to make brain processing more efficient.

So, if you aren't learning a foreign language, for example, you aren't using that synaptic pathway and that pathway will be pruned away. That doesn't mean that you can never learn a foreign language again, it just means that it will be harder for you to learn a foreign language than it would have been when you were a kid. You may have noticed this—generally, little kids are able to learn foreign languages more quickly than adults.

And likewise, if you are using a particular pathway a lot, those neuronal pathways will be strengthened—like if you play a sport, the pathways needed to play that sport, like coordination, will grow stronger. Because the brain is going through this process of pruning and strengthening of nerve pathways, it's particularly sensitive to everything you do at this stage. So any activities that you do or don't do when you're a teen affect your brain development.

Another change that happens during the teen years is that the neurons in your brain get covered with what's called a "myelin sheath." This fatty sheath helps the neurons send messages back and forth to your brain more quickly and efficiently—in fact, a hundred times faster. And the resting period between firing messages is thirty times faster. This means that messages that are transmitted after myelination occur three thousand times faster than those before myelination! This whole process of pruning and myelination is to make the brain more coordinated and efficient.

At the same time, the prefrontal cortex of your brain—the part responsible for planning, making decisions, and thinking logically—begins to undergo more rapid development at around age eleven or twelve, and is changing all through the teen years, and doesn't finish developing until about age twenty-five. It's getting you ready for all those adult-type decisions that you'll need to do when you're an adult.

And the limbic system, the emotional center of your brain—the part that becomes activated when you're afraid or feel that you have to protect yourself—also starts changing at the same time, around age eleven or twelve. But it's pretty much finished developing when you're fifteen or sixteen. So if you've noticed that you're more emotional in your teen years than you were before, that's why—the emotional center of your brain is fully developed, and your logical thinking part isn't. Since the logical thinking part—the prefrontal cortex—is what "calms down" the emotional part, it can't do that very well if it's not yet well-developed.

So, naturally, your emotions can feel pretty out of control at times! But have no fear, the prefrontal cortex will eventually catch up, and all will once again be in balance in that remarkable brain of yours.

This is all to say that your brain is going through all kinds of changes in your teen years, which naturally affect your emotions and behavior. So, as your brain is getting you ready to be an adult, your attitude and behavior reflect those changes. Your parents and family may take on less of a central role, and your peer group—where you will eventually find someone to have kids with, and hence continue the species—becomes more important.

I know what you're thinking—not everyone has kids, and your life isn't all about having kids. There's a whole lot more that you plan to do. Of course, this is true, but from the viewpoint of biology and evolution, continuing the species is what it's all about. Mother Nature has designed this system to ensure that this species that she's designed—us—survives.

So, friend groups become super important, because we need them to survive, and anything that happens that excludes you from a friend group makes you feel super threatened, hurt, and scared.

• *Leila's Story*

Leila thought she had a great group of friends. True, on occasion someone got mad at someone else for some reason and then they were cut out of the group. But this had never happened to her.

Until now.

It started like any other evening—Leila was sitting on her bed doing her homework, with her phone nearby. From time to time she'd get bored with her algebra and pick up her phone, to see if there was anything new and exciting going on. At one point, she noticed that one of her friends had posted a photo of a bunch of her other friends hanging out at someone's house, and they looked like they were having a ton of fun.

Without her.

They were all there—her whole crowd. Naturally, Leila wondered why she hadn't been invited. Did she say something that made someone upset? She heard the familiar voice of her inner critic emerge: "What did you do this time?"

She felt her heart sinking. She felt confused—and very alone. And the worst part was the not knowing—not knowing what was going on, not knowing why she hadn't been included.

But luckily for Leila, she had taken a self-compassion class, and she remembered what to do.

First, she gave herself some supportive touch—she put her hand on her heart and made small circles with her hand over her heart. She remembered that bringing attention to physical sensations would allow the story in her mind—the story about how she must have hurt one of her friends, or how they simply decided that they didn't like her—to fade. But the story would sneak back in again from time to time, and when it did, she would remind herself that "Thoughts are not facts," and she would come back to feeling the warmth of her hand on her heart. The physical sensation of soothing circles on her heart—the warmth, the supportive touch—helped her feel a little better.

Leila was able to then ask herself the fundamental self-compassion question: What is it that I need right now? What do I need to hear?

When she did this, and took time to listen, she heard words arising—from someplace deep inside her, her own true voice. The words that came up for her were quiet and soft, almost a whisper: "You are loved." With her hand still on her heart, she silently repeated to herself, "You are loved…you are loved…you are loved."

And then another thought came to her, something else that she needed to hear: "You are awesome, just the way you are." So she repeated this to herself silently for a few minutes. "You are awesome just the way you are." Leila was able to calm down enough to eventually return to her algebra.

But from time to time, the thought of that photo would pop into her head, and she'd get the sickening feeling again in the pit of her stomach. When this happened, she returned to her physical sensations— her hand on her heart—or the words that she needed to hear.

Leila recalled that identifying feelings and naming them would engage the prefrontal cortex of her brain, which would calm down the emotion center, the limbic system. She thought she'd try it. What is it that I'm feeling? Hurt, anger, loneliness… Which is the strongest? It took a few minutes to decide, because all three emotions were definitely present. She finally decided that it seemed like anger was

*rising to the surface. Leila named it with a soft voice,
saying, "Anger, Leila, this is anger. This is what anger feels
like." And then another thought came to her: "Anger is a
normal human emotion. All of us feel anger at some time or
another."*

*She scanned her body to see where the anger resided.
When she got to her stomach, it was clear—that was where
it was. A huge heavy weight somewhere in the depths of
her stomach. She remembered to soften and open to the
feeling, imagining it softening first like playdough and
then, as it loosened a bit, like cake batter; she encircled it
with warmth, giving it lots of space simply to be there. Not
resisting the feeling or pushing it away. Leila noticed that it
soon began to lose energy, to weaken.*

*Once again, Leila returned to her homework. When
distracting thoughts came up, or she noticed strong
emotions like anger arising, she would return to her
practice of naming the emotion, finding it in her body, and
then softening and opening to it.*

Dealing with Anger

I don't have to tell you that anger is a strong emotion. Experiencing anger is part of the experience of being human. Some people have the impression that anger is bad—but it's really only negative if it leads to actions that hurt others or yourself. Sometimes it can be good—if it leads you to take action to fight injustice or stand up for yourself. Being angry has led many to fight for civil rights, to end slavery and engage in many other social movements.

However, anger is considered an outer, hard emotion that covers and protects a softer, more vulnerable emotion. And it's precisely because that softer emotion makes you feel vulnerable that you develop anger in the first place—to protect yourself from being hurt further.

What do I mean by softer emotions? Loneliness, hurt, fear, disappointment, sadness, and grief are examples of softer, more vulnerable emotions. Often when we're feeling these feelings, we get angry, because it feels like the strength of anger protects us from feeling the painful softer emotions. Anger gives us a sense of power and a shield so that we don't get hurt again.

But there are a couple of problems with the way this works. One is that in order to really *heal* from the hurt, or the grief, or the sadness that we're experiencing, we have to allow ourselves to *feel* the emotion, and anger doesn't let us do that. It stands in the way. The other problem is that anger doesn't feel good. When we're feeling angry, we might think that we're getting back at the person that we're angry at, as if our anger is magically sending poison arrows through the sky that mysteriously land in the heart of the person we're angry at. But let's face it, the person we're angry at can be completely oblivious to our anger, while we suffer with this awful feeling that anger brings.

But sometimes we're just not ready to open up, to feel our vulnerability and our hurt. Sometimes we need protection, at least for a little while, until we are ready to be with our pain. That's fine—there's no rush, and it's okay to be angry, as long as you're not hurting anyone, including yourself.

When you are ready to move on from the anger and explore it a little, you can do this practice.

Exercise: Exploring Anger and Meeting Unmet Needs

You can download audio for this exercise at http://www.newharbinger.com/45274.

For this exercise, you'll need a pen and paper.

- Close your eyes and think about the situation that is making you feel angry. Check in with yourself to see if you are ready to let you anger go. Is the anger causing you discomfort? Are you tired of feeling angry? Is constantly being angry exhausting you? Is the anger not serving you anymore? And just so you know, letting go of anger doesn't mean that you're saying that the person was right—you can still believe that you were right and they were wrong—it just means that you're ready to move on from it.

- If you think that you're ready to let go of this anger, write down some notes about the situation.

- Know that it's completely natural for you to feel the way you do. Perhaps say to yourself, "Of course you're angry, it was very hurtful! You have a right to be angry!"

- Sometimes we hold on to anger because we don't want to feel other feelings. Consider that perhaps there are other feelings, softer feelings, that maybe the anger might be covering up, like sadness, loneliness, hurt, or maybe shame or embarrassment. Take a moment to explore what other more vulnerable feelings might be underneath the anger. Write these softer feelings down.

- Close your eyes again and consider for a moment what you might have needed in this situation. What was it that you needed that you didn't get? Maybe you needed to be heard, or seen, or recognized. Maybe you needed to feel like you belonged, or to feel connected, like a part of a group. Remember that whatever you are feeling is natural. All teens—and adults too—have needs! If you find something that you needed and didn't get, write it down.

- If you'd like, put your hand over your heart, offering yourself some supportive touch, giving yourself some kindness and warmth. These feelings are not easy. We are not trying to make them go away, we are simply meeting them with a little warmth, kindness, and understanding.

- Now perhaps you can meet your own needs directly. For example:

  - If you felt unseen, can you try telling yourself "I see you?"

  - If you felt alone, can tell yourself "I'm here for you?"

  - If you felt unloved, can you tell yourself "I love you?"

- In other words, can you give to yourself right now what you were hoping to receive from others? Can you say the words to yourself that you really needed to hear? You can try whispering this to yourself silently, slowly, hearing the words that are coming from your own true voice.

- When you're ready, you can gently open your eyes.

After this practice, notice how you're feeling. You may notice a slight shift in your emotions—there may be a subtle sense of a little less anger, or that the anger doesn't have the energy that it once did. Like maybe you just don't care as much about being angry.

Changes don't usually happen all at once, and these exercises and meditations aren't some magic pill. Rather, doing these exercises opens the door to begin the process of letting go of your anger. And then bit by bit, little by little, you may notice your attitude about this person or the situation shift. Then one day, you may realize you're simply not angry anymore...that it's not worth your energy to even think about getting angry.

Relationships with Parents

Friends aren't the only ones you might feel angry at. Just about all teens say that they get super angry at their parents from time to time.

Relationships with parents usually change in your teen years. Parents may suddenly seem extremely uncool, or downright annoying. Or like they have no idea who you are, how you've changed, and what you're about.

• *Zoe's Story*

Zoe used to get along pretty well with her parents. But lately there have been a lot of conflicts at home, and so Zoe's parents thought it was a good idea for her to start seeing a therapist. This is what she told her therapist:

"Spending time with my parents didn't use to be so bad. But now all of a sudden, they've become super strict. I have to give them my cell phone at nine at night. Nine p.m.!! That's just when my friends really start chatting and posting. And because I'm excluded from all that conversation, the next day at school I have no idea what's going on, and I feel really left out. On top of that, my mom won't let me start dating until I'm fifteen. That's crazy—I have friends who are dating now, and fifteen is two years away. And then my dad is super crazy when it comes to what clothes I can wear. I mean, of course, he doesn't care about fashion at all, and won't let me wear clothes that are

fashionable, like jeans with holes in them or short skirts. And just forget about any tattoos or piercings. Those are out of the question."

What has changed? Why does it appear that Zoe's parents have become more restrictive, just when Zoe is beginning to develop her own ideas and her own style? Why won't they just let her be herself?

To understand what's going on, it helps to know what the "job" of parents and the "job" of teens are in the teen years.

First, the parents' job. Most parents or caregivers, at least those with good intentions, feel that their job is to keep their kids safe. This means that their decisions are based on what they think will keep them alive, out of trouble, and healthy.

Now, teens' job. The job of teens is to figure out how they want to be in the world. This means finding out what's important to them, which will eventually lead them to figure out a career or vocation and what kind of people they want to spend their life with. To do this, they have to do some exploring—maybe trying out different fashions or style of dress, perhaps experimenting with different activities and friend groups, and possibly even taking some risks. For some, it might even mean taking some risks that aren't so healthy.

And here's where the conflict comes in: parents want to keep you safe, and you want to try new things—some of which parents might consider risky. You might not think they're risky, but your parents might—they love you and have heard all the stories where teens meet some person online and then arrange to meet them in person and end up getting cut up into a thousand pieces and stuck in some freezer somewhere. Yeah, yeah, I know that's not going to happen to you, but parents are terrified. It is a fear, reasonable or not, that most parents have.

So how can parents and teens work together to overcome some of these conflicts? How can they remember to see the other as simply someone who is also trying to figure out how to move ahead with the least conflict possible? Remember the "A Person Just Like Me" practice from chapter 2? This time, instead of thinking of some random person, bring to mind a parent or caregiver who is making you a little crazy.

Meditation: A Person Just like Me— Parent or Caregiver

You can download audio for this meditation at
http://www.newharbinger.com/45274.

- First, sit in a comfortable place and take a few deep, slow breaths, allowing yourself to feel the movement of your inhale and the movement of your exhale with each breath. Take your time.

- Now, bring an image of your parent or caregiver to mind. Think of them in as much detail as you can—and for now, you can imagine them at a comfortable distance away from you—whatever feels right.

- Repeat the following words slowly to yourself as you think of your parent or caregiver. It's really important that you don't rush through the phrases, but take your time so that the words can really sink in. As you say them, think about their meaning.

  - *My mom/dad/caregiver [choose whichever feels appropriate] is a human being, just like me.*

  - *My mom/dad/caregiver has a body and a mind, just like me.*

  - *My mom/dad/caregiver has feelings, emotions, and thoughts, just like me.*

  - *My mom/dad/caregiver has, at some point, been sad, disappointed, angry, hurt, or confused, just like me.*

  - *My mom/dad/caregiver wishes to be free from pain and unhappiness, just like me.*

  - *My mom/dad/caregiver wishes to be safe, healthy, and loved, just like me.*

  - *My mom/dad/caregiver wishes to be happy, just like me.*

- Now let's allow some wishes for this person to arise:

  - *I wish for my mom/dad/caregiver to have the strength, resources, and support to help him/her through the difficult times in life.*

- *I wish for my mom/dad/caregiver to be free from pain and suffering.*

- *I wish for my mom/dad/caregiver to be strong and balanced.*

- *I wish for my mom/dad/caregiver to be happy because she/he is a human being, just like me.*

• Take a few more deep breaths and notice what you're feeling.

• When you're ready, gently open your eyes.

Were you surprised by anything that came up for you? You may have noticed some slight shifts in how you feel about this person. Whatever you are feeling, just simply allow the feelings to be there, without pushing them away. You don't have to do anything with the feelings—simply make space for them. You may want to put a hand on your heart or another soothing place and give yourself a little compassion.

Sometimes you may be experiencing so much frustration or anger that you aren't able to practice "A Person Just Like Me." If this is the case, it might be best to start with the following practice. You can follow it with "A Person Just Like Me" if you then feel ready to do that.

Exercise: Self-Compassion Sunbath

You can download audio for this exercise at
http://www.newharbinger.com/45274.

- First, sit in a comfortable position, and take a few breaths to simply allow yourself to settle and relax. With each exhale, let go of a little of the stress and tension in your body—letting go a little more with each exhale.

- Next, imagine you're on a beautiful exotic beach. In front of you is the ocean—a deep green-blue color, against the cloudless light blue sky. You lay down on the sand, and feel the warmth of the sun on your skin. You can feel your skin soaking up the warmth of the sun, almost like a sponge. The warmth is perfect—not too hot, just enough so that it feels just right against your skin. In fact, it's just what you need right now.

- As you lie here, you notice that there seems to be a feeling coming with the warmth—a feeling that envelops you, holds you, supports you. It's a feeling of overwhelming calmness, a knowingness, a sense of peace. And you hear some words—or maybe not hear, exactly, but simply know in the core of your being—that are simply this: "Everything is going to be okay." Somehow, deep in your bones, you know this to be true. You know that whatever happens, however things work out, all will be okay.

- You lie on the sand, feeling the warmth of the sun permeating your body, offering you a deep sense of peace, of unconditional acceptance, and an inner knowledge that all will be well.

- You can stay here for as long as you like. And when you're ready, gently open your eyes.

Notice how you feel when this practice is over, and know that you can return and take a self-compassion sunbath whenever you like.

Conclusion

Much of the unhappiness and feelings of unworthiness during the teen years come from difficulties in relationships. Relationships shift and changes take place that are rooted in evolution and in our biology. Learning skills to deal with the self-criticism that may result when relationships become painful can do a lot to help ease the pain. These practices help you let go of the incessant stories about who's right and who's wrong that seem to take over our minds when we feel engulfed in emotion.

In particular, when we're angry, these practices help us to see underneath our anger, to the softer feelings and unmet needs that lie below. When we have the courage to do this, we can hear our own true voice, the compassionate voice that tells us that everything will be okay, and that we are fine just the way we are.

In the next chapter, we'll face another aspect of teens' lives that also causes a lot of pain—how you look and how you feel about how you look. If your appearance has ever caused you any feelings of insecurity or caused you to be hard on yourself, turn the page...

CHAPTER 8

Making Peace with Your Self-Image

Teens, in particular, are often highly sensitive about their image and how they look. You might hate how your hair looks, or the color of your eyes or the shape of your nose. Maybe you think your lips are too fat or thin. Maybe you're self-conscious about the acne on your cheeks or how your biceps look in your T-shirt. You might spend countless hours in front of the mirror trying to get your nose/chin/legs/eyes to look the way you want them to.

Wanting things to be different than they are, whether it's how we look or some other aspect of our lives, causes us a lot of suffering and pain.

There are some things in life that we don't have a lot of control over. One of those things is how we look. Sure, we can change our hairstyle, work out and change our body shape, wear different clothes, put on makeup, but fundamentally the features that we have are our features, and unless we invest in plastic surgery, they aren't going to change much.

Unfortunately, not liking how you look and wanting to look different is not going to help you feel better. In fact, it is guaranteed to make you feel worse—to lead you to more struggle and more unhappiness. Finding a way to accept how you look and making the best of what you have will be much more gratifying to you in the long run.

So how do you get there? How do you get to the point where you can actually accept and love who you are, including how you look and how you feel about your body?

First, have patience. You've probably spent a lot of time disliking what you look like, so this isn't going to change overnight. It will happen slowly, but I promise you that you will get there. One day you'll wake up and realize that it's actually interesting that your smile is a little crooked. It's kind of cute.

Second, let's think about why you dislike what you look like and parts of your body. Chances are it's because you don't look like the "ideal"—like the images that you've seen in advertising, on TV, in movies, or on social media. That's a bit of a problem, because we know that those images aren't real—comparing your very real face and body to one that has been extensively altered or filtered is more than a bit unfair to you.

We've been fed this idea by our media and culture—not only about how we're supposed to look, but also about how we're supposed to be. How we're supposed to act. Or, more specifically, how we're supposed to act if we're female and how we're supposed to act if we're male. And this is a problem.

Toxic Masculinity

"Be a man!"

Most boys are told this at some point during their youth. Some boys are told this continually as they are growing up. What does it mean, anyway?

It means to not show when you're hurt; to not express emotions—especially any emotions that could be interpreted as soft, like fear or sadness; to be tough; and most important, to never cry. The end result of receiving this message over time is something called toxic masculinity—which, in addition to not sharing vulnerable or soft feelings, means being aggressive to the point of being violent, in order to show how powerful you are, particularly over girls. The belief here is that being violent means that you're powerful, and being powerful means that you're worth something.

Raising boys with this belief—that a man is only worthy if he is powerful and violent—leads them to become men who think they have a right, or even an obligation, to dominate women. These men often have trouble determining when they are hurting emotionally, don't know how to manage their painful feelings, and can't recognize when they need help. These men aren't secure in just being themselves, and so they feel that they constantly have to prove themselves—prove that they are worthy. Some researchers think that men's shorter life spans and greater heart disease has to do with the stress that they are under by having to constantly prove themselves, while at the same time trying hard to keep their painful emotions concealed.

Clearly, our society and cultural expectations need to change so that boys are raised to become men who are able to be themselves, feel and express their full range of emotions, and relate to both women and men as equals, without feeling like they have to show that they are stronger or more powerful than anyone else. But until then, how can self-compassion help?

Self-compassion teaches us that we are worthy just as we are. That we don't have to be better than others to be valuable and valued, and that we can be ourselves—human flaws and all—and make a positive difference in others' lives and in the world. Contrary to the message that "Be a man" carries, self-compassion says to "Be yourself." Self-compassion says that you are great just the way you are, and you don't have to prove yourself to anyone. You can be happy, content, relaxed, at peace with who you are, without any need to compare yourself to anyone else. A kind of radical thought, right? It is possible, but only probable if we start with ourselves.

And the good news is that you have a choice. You can allow some unhealthy external ideal or message control how you feel about yourself, or you can learn to accept and love yourself as you are, with your strengths and weaknesses. You can let someone else tell you who you are, and who you should be, or you can simply be who you are, with your own unique style, look, and sense of self. You can be brave enough to be you. You can do this by embracing who you are and accepting what you look like—including parts of your body and image that you might not like.

Embracing Myself

You might be thinking, *Yeah, sounds great, but how do I get there? I'd love to be okay with my body and who I am, but I'm so far from that now...*

The following practice will help you get started with accepting your body. It's called a body scan. Not only can it help you learn to love and appreciate yourself as you are, it's also super relaxing.

This particular version of a body scan has been modified for teens, and to emphasize allowing us to be with whatever sensations are here and whatever emotions come up when we do this practice—a step toward being brave enough to be yourself.

It's best to approach this exercise with an attitude of simply experimenting with it– you're trying out this practice to see what it's like. And remember that if parts of it feel a bit uncomfortable, you have a choice: you can see if you can be brave and open up to the uncomfortable feelings—allowing them to be there, with a sense of gentleness, tenderness, and kindness, like the attitude you might have if you were holding a newborn puppy. Or if you don't feel like challenging yourself at this moment—and that's totally okay; remember, self-compassion is about giving yourself what you need—you can skip the part of the body that's causing discomfort and go on to another part.

Another way to do this practice is to do only a part of it at a time. You can just do the part at the beginning, which focuses on your legs, or the part about your belly and chest, or you can do the part about your face and head. Or you can switch it up, and do one part one day, and another part another day. It's always your choice.

Self-Compassionate Body Scan

You can download audio for this meditation at http://www.newharbinger.com/45274.

- Get comfortable. You may want to lie down on your back and close your eyes. Your arms can rest by your sides naturally if that feels comfortable for you, and your legs can relax. If you'd like, you can put a cushion or pillow under your knees—some people feel really supported like that. Also, you can put your head on a pillow if that works for you, but be careful—you don't want to fall asleep, because then you would miss the whole practice!

- Now bring your attention to your breath, seeing if you can simply notice as it moves gently in and out of your body. Notice your belly rising and falling with each in-breath and each out-breath. You're not trying to change your breath in any way, you're just noticing it being there, doing its thing.

- If it feels comfortable for you, you can do some supportive touch—maybe placing a hand on your heart to remind yourself that you are here, and, as a human being alive and breathing on this planet, you are deserving of care and kindness. Just like a newborn puppy. Or maybe stroking your face or cradling your face in your hands. Feeling the warmth of your hand on your chest, or your hands on your face, take three deep, slow, relaxing breaths. When you are ready, you can place your arm by your side again or stay with your supportive touch.

- Now, shift your attention all the way down through your body to the soles of your feet. Simply notice any sensations in the soles of your feet. Are they warm or cool, dry or moist? Can you feel the place where your toes might be touching each other? Can you feel the contact point where your heels touch the surface of the floor or the couch? Notice what that point of contact feels like—if it's hard, soft, or maybe you feel some pressure.

- Take a moment to consider everything your feet do for you all day long. Your feet have such a small surface area, yet they hold up your entire body! Imagine how much work that is for them. Our feet do all of that and more—although we rarely pay any attention to them. So take a moment, for the next few breaths, to appreciate your feet, which make it possible for you to go from one place to another.

- Shift your attention from your feet up into your ankles, calves, and shins. Notice any sensations that you might be feeling in your lower legs. Perhaps you notice the texture of clothing on your skin. If so, see what that texture feels like. Is it scratchy or smooth? Velvety or rough? Maybe something in between?

- At some point you will notice that your mind has wandered, and you are no longer noticing sensations but are thinking about something else. When this happens, simply return your attention to the sensations in your body.

- Now, returning to your legs, shift your attention up through your knees, to your thighs and hips. Again, notice what is here in the way of sensation. Maybe there's a slight tickling from the fabric of your clothing, or maybe scratchiness or warmth.

- At some point, you might notice thoughts arising like *I don't like this part of my body, it's too fat* or maybe *It's too skinny* or *It's not muscular enough.* If you notice these thoughts arising, see if you can muster up a little bravery and stay with that part of your body, keeping your attention there and breathing in a little bit of extra love for that part of your body. As crazy as it may sound, you can even talk to this body part, and say something like "I'm glad you're here and that you help my body work!" Then you can move on to the next body part. Alternatively, if you're not feeling too brave today, it's fine to skip it and just move to a different body part. You can always come back when you feel ready. Remember, you're in charge.

- Bringing your attention now to your belly, be aware of your belly moving—expanding and contracting with each breath. Notice any feelings that might arise as you pay attention to your belly. Are there feelings of dislike, pushing away, or not wanting to stay with this body part or these feelings? If so, see if you can turn toward these feelings—pay attention to them, and notice what they actually feel like. You may feel some sensations in your body that are associated with those feelings. See if you can stay with those sensations for a few minutes. Again, you might want to say a few kind words to yourself. Maybe some words of encouragement, like "Wow, you're being super brave to stay with these difficult feelings" or some kind words that you might say to a good friend, like "I'm so sorry you feel this way. I promise this won't last forever," or even "I know how hard my stomach works to digest my food. I'm sorry I've been so hard on it!"

- If you'd like, you can put your hand on your belly and gently rub it in a soothing way.

- And now, shifting your attention to the chest, notice your lungs expanding with each breath, and your chest rising and falling.

Maybe you notice the beating of your heart—this heart that has been beating all your life, even before you were born! It's been beating only for you, its whole reason for existing is to keep you alive. See if you can take a moment to feel some appreciation for these lungs and this heart for all the work they do.

- Now move your attention to your neck, throat, and head. Aware of the strength of this neck that supports your head, holds it up all day long, allow yourself to feel thankfulness for it. And this throat that allows you to talk, to swallow, and to breathe. Your head and skull that keep your brain safe, your eyes that see, your nose that breathes, your mouth that eats, your ears that hear, and your lips that speak. Their job is to make it possible for you to communicate, to nourish yourself, to see and appreciate the world, to think, to create, to express yourself. Take a moment now to silently say some words of appreciation for all these parts of your body, and how they function to keep you alive and engaged in this world.

- Perhaps you've come across a part of your face that you're not so happy with. Perhaps you think your nose is too big or your eyes are too small. Maybe you've noticed some thoughts arising like *I wish my ears didn't stick out* or *I wish I didn't have such bad acne*. Along with those thoughts may be feelings—maybe a sinking feeling or even outright disgust. Maybe you can be brave and open to those feelings, allowing them to be here, allowing yourself to feel whatever you're feeling, and simply be who you are.

- And while you are opening to these feelings, bring a softening to them. Imagine a warm washcloth on your face, allowing the muscles of your face to relax. Maybe even imagine someone giving you a gentle face massage, someone with loving hands gently touching your face and helping the muscles to relax and let go.

- Consider silently whispering some kind words to yourself—words like "I'm so sorry you feel this way about your body" or "It's hard having those feelings about your face" or "I know you've felt this way a long time…that must be so hard to feel criticized like this." You might want to do some supportive touch—perhaps putting a hand on your heart, stroking your cheek, or giving yourself a hug. Stay here for as long as you need to, feeling the gentle comfort of your hug and your kind words.

- When you are ready, gently open your eyes. Take a moment to wiggle your fingers and toes, then your hands, wrists, and feet. Stretch your body however it feels like it needs to be stretched, turn over on your side, and push yourself up.

Keep in mind: This is an experiment. We're seeing what it's like when we pay attention to our physical sensations and our thoughts and feelings. Once we notice what's here, we can see if we can stay with the feeling, maybe opening to it, making space for it, and then bringing a little tenderness to this area. Remember, being with difficult feelings is hard, so it's important to be kind to yourself.

Resisting Your Body

When practicing the body scan, perhaps there were parts of your body that made you feel uncomfortable, where you didn't want to stay and feel sensations. Maybe there were parts of your body that you genuinely didn't like.

When we resist, or push away parts of ourselves, the feelings that emerge from these parts persist. In other words, we can't escape these feelings by pushing them away. *What we resist, persists.*

The body scan practice can help us to learn how to face these uncomfortable feelings. What does it mean to face these feelings? It means not resisting them. It means allowing them to be here, allowing yourself to feel them, making space for them, and being with them with an attitude of tenderness and care. Remember holding that newborn puppy? Just like that.

It takes bravery to be with feelings that are uncomfortable. I mean, really, who wants to do that? It's not fun. But it allows you to open up to yourself, and with time you will find that "yourself" is truly lovable. Acne and all.

And remember the expression we mentioned earlier: *What you feel, you can heal.* So allowing yourself to feel whatever you are feeling, rather than pushing the feelings away, helps you to be comfortable with your true self.

• Betina's Story

Betina was convinced that she was ugly, and would never be remotely attractive. When she was about eleven years old, her classmates started teasing her about the size of her nose. Before that, she had never noticed anything different about her nose, but once kids started teasing her, she became very self-conscious about it. Now she was fifteen, and kids still commented on it from time to time. They thought it was funny, and didn't realize how much it upset Betina. Because of this, Betina knew, without a doubt, that there was no way anyone would ever think that she was nice-looking.

When Betina did the body scan, she was fine until she got to her face—and in particular, her nose. When she tried to be appreciative for her nose—it did allow her to smell and enjoy food, after all—she found herself just getting angry. At first, the words she heard in her head were, It's not fair that I have this nose! I didn't ask for it! Why can't I have one of those cute button noses?

Then she remembered that wanting things to be different than they are causes more suffering, more struggle. And she remembered that in mindfulness practice she was taught to observe her thoughts, and allow them to drift away. She then realized that what was there once the thoughts drifted away was sadness—sadness that she was given this nose that she wasn't happy with, and had to go through life with it.

Her mindfulness and self-compassion practice had taught her to be open to the feelings that were present at that moment. At first, she didn't want to do this, because she didn't want to feel the sadness that was there. But at that particular moment, she felt that she had enough courage within her to manage it, and so she said to herself, calmly and gently, "Sadness, this is sadness. I'm feeling sad right now."

Betina then felt an urge to leave the sad feelings and go back to thinking about how unfair it was that she was stuck with this nose. It was easier to be angry than to feel sad—but she decided to see if she could stay with the sad feeling. Just for another moment. Allowing it to be present, noticing how it felt in her body, observing it, but also not dwelling in it. Just feeling it.

Then a surprising thing happened. Betina realized that her nose was just a nose. Okay, maybe a bigger than usual nose, but it was just a nose—it no longer seemed like this huge source of angst and anger and emotional pain anymore. It was simply a feature in the middle of her face—sitting between her eyes and her mouth. That's it.

Hello Again, Inner Critic

When it comes to our attitude about how we look and what we think about our bodies, for many of us the inner critic is alive, well, and thriving. Many of us have super strong critical voices in our heads, saying things like "You're so ugly. Why would anyone like you?" or "You're so big and fat. Of course no one is going to want to date you!" This incessant voice makes us feel unworthy, less than, and overall, pretty discouraged.

How can we quiet this critical inner voice? How can we learn to be kinder to ourselves, especially when it comes to our own self-image?

It might be helpful to see why that inner critical voice exists in the first place. Often, that voice is there to protect us in some way. For example, part of us might be afraid of being rejected by others, so if the inner critic says something like "No one will like you!" it beats the would-be rejector to the punch. In other words, we're prepared and not caught off guard when someone really does reject us, because we've already rejected ourselves.

Another thing the inner critic achieves by putting us down—especially when it happens in front of others—is that it makes others see that we don't think that we're better than them. Especially among girls, it seems that putting yourself down is equivalent to saying "I know I'm not any better than you. We're all in this together." It's a way of connecting with others, as if you're establishing an agreement of sorts, that you aren't going to outdo anyone and that you're all on the same team. We know from an evolutionary perspective, being on a team rather than going at it solo helps us survive—the group can help protect you.

So in relation to your attitude and the words you say to yourself about how you look and what you think about your body, the inner critic is often trying to keep you safe and protected. However, at times it can go a bit overboard, and this is when stress and depression can set in. But there's a way you can keep this critical inner voice in check.

In the next exercise, in which you'll need paper and something to write with, you will learn how to quiet the voice of the inner critic when it becomes overbearing in relation to your looks. This allows space for a new voice to emerge—one which is also yours, but much kinder and more compassionate.

Quieting the Inner Critic and Hearing Your Own True Voice

You can download audio for this meditation at http://www.newharbinger.com/45274.

- Think of something about your appearance that you continually beat yourself up about. It might be that you think your ears stick out or your nose is too big.

- Now write down what the inner critic in you typically says when you notice this part of yourself that you're not happy with. How does your inner critic express itself, and what tone does it use? For example, does it say things like "You have the nose of a giant. You are never, ever going to look decent, let alone attractive."

- Now think about how much suffering your inner critic has caused you so far. Try giving yourself compassion for how hard it is to continually hear such harsh criticism. A good way to do this is to write yourself some kind words. For example, you might write:

  - *I'm so sorry you've had to hear these harsh words for so long.*

  - *You don't deserve this. You are a truly beautiful person inside!*

  - *I love you and want you to be happy!*

- Or you might even want to offer yourself a supportive touch— maybe a hand on your heart, a pat on your back, or a gentle hug.

- Now think about this: Is it possible that the inner critic is trying to *protect* you in some way, to keep you safe, even if it's unproductive or hurts you along the way? Maybe it's trying to protect you from being hurt by someone else?

  - If so, please write down how your inner critic might be trying to keep you safe, protected from some perceived risk or danger to you.

  - If you have identified some way your inner critic might be trying to keep you safe, see if you can acknowledge that effort by your inner critic—write down a few words of thanks. Let the inner critic know that even though it may not be serving you very well now, its intention was good, and it was trying its best.

- If you can't find any way that the inner critic is trying to help you— sometimes the criticism seems to have no value whatsoever— continue to give yourself compassion for how you've suffered by being self-critical in the past.

- Now that we've heard from one part of you, the Inner Critic, let's find another voice inside you. This voice is usually quieter and gentler, but emerges when you are still and listen closely. This voice is wise, loves you completely, and wants the best for you.

- Close your eyes and place your hands over your heart if that feels right for you. Now, speaking from the wise and compassionate part, say to yourself:

  - "I love you and want the best for you. I know how hard it is hearing this harsh criticism about a part of you. I'm sorry that you've had to hear that for so long! Especially since this is a time when you are going through so many changes. Changes in your brain, changes in your body, changes in relationships with friends and with family. Pressures at school. So much is going on. So how about being kind and gentle with yourself, okay?"

  - "I love you and I don't want you to struggle anymore! What can I say to help you feel better?"

  - "Your inner being—the essence of who you are—is beautiful. You know deep inside that this is true!"

- If you have a hard time coming up with words to say that ring true for you, try thinking of what a really good friend or even your pet might say as a way of comforting you. Pets love us no matter how we look or what mistakes we make—and they often sense our discomfort and comfort us just when we need it most. So imagine what they might say if they could talk. Maybe they might say something like, "I care about you and I'm here to protect you and take care of you."

  - Take some time to silently repeat these kind words to yourself.

- Now from the wise, compassionate voice, your own true voice, you might want to write a letter to yourself, expressing how those harsh, critical words aren't serving you and perhaps next time you could offer yourself a kind message instead.

If you have trouble finding the right words to say to encourage yourself, don't worry—this takes time, and will become easier with practice. The important thing is to set your intention to try to be kinder to yourself.

Note that in this exercise we gave the inner critical voice space. We allowed it to be present, even thanking it for trying to keep you safe all these years. If we had banished it, or pushed it away, it would come back even stronger. Allowing these difficult feelings to be present actually makes them less powerful. And being still and listening allows our own true voice to emerge.

Don't be discouraged if you keep hearing from that inner critic from time to time. Remember, it's trying to keep us safe, and so will pop its head out occasionally. That's fine. You always can choose how much or how little to listen to it.

Conclusion

We are constantly subject to the message from advertising and the media that we aren't attractive, popular, or good enough. We compare ourselves to others and end up feeling like we just don't measure up.

But there is a way out—it is possible to let go of the critical voice that tells you that you're not good enough, and listen to your own true voice, often buried deep within you, that tells you you're lovable, and good enough just as you are. It will guide you if you listen.

CHAPTER 9

Navigating Your LGBTQIA+ Identity

Being a teen is all about figuring out who you are. It's a journey that involves a deep dive into finding out what is truly important to you, what gives your life meaning, and how you want to be in the world. For many teens, this means exploring their sexual and gender identities. Even if you are cisgender, meaning that you identify as the gender that you were assigned when you were born, or heterosexual, meaning that you're only attracted to the opposite gender, you may still benefit from reading this chapter. For one, this chapter deals with shame, which is an emotion that arises in all of us, whether or not we are LGBTQIA+. So you may find it helpful to learn about shame and do the exercise that shows you how to give yourself compassion when shame comes up.

Before diving into this chapter, it's important that we differentiate "gender identity" from "sexual identity." Gender identity refers to the gender you consider yourself to be. This can be everything from boy to girl, or neither. Although, in our Western culture, most of us have been raised to believe there are only two genders—male and female—many cultures across history have honored three, four, and even five genders. Many Native American tribes have several genders, for example, as do the Kathoey in Thailand, the Salzikrum of the Middle East, the Hijra caste in India, and the Fa'afafine of Samoa, to name a few (Testa, Coolhart, and Peta, 2015).

Today, in the US and worldwide, there are many who consider themselves nonbinary, which means neither male or female. Our society is just beginning to understand that gender can be a continuum from man to woman and everything in between. In years to come, the idea of a gender continuum will likely be much more understood and accepted, but until then those who are nonbinary often struggle with feeling like outsiders, or even like there is something wrong with them, because of the messages they receive from our society.

Sexual identity is a completely different thing; it refers to who you are attracted to. For example, you can be a man and attracted to a women (heterosexual), or a man attracted to other men (gay). You can also be a woman and attracted to men (heterosexual), or a woman and attracted to other women (lesbian). You could also be bisexual, attracted to both men and women, or queer or pansexual, attracted to people independent of gender. Having a sexual identity other than heterosexual, in general, is more accepted these days, but many teens who are exploring their sexual identity, or consider themselves gay, still may struggle with feeling different or like they don't belong.

Every culture has a set of norms—certain things we have been raised to believe are "normal." If we're outside of those norms, we can feel like there's something wrong with us. And unfortunately, these norms are often pretty narrow, so for a lot of people it's hard to fit into them. And when we don't fit in, we often feel shame.

• *Santi's Story*

Santi was raised as a boy, but was never comfortable with being a boy. Today, Santi identifies as a girl and asks that people refer to her using she/her/hers pronouns. I will therefore use those pronouns in describing Santi's experience, even when talking about Santi before she started her gender transition.

As a young child, Santi didn't enjoy most typical boy activities, preferring to play with her sister's dolls and dress up in her sister's princess gowns. When Santi was four, she announced to her parents that she was a girl, and wanted to wear dresses to preschool and grow long hair. Santi's parents weren't comfortable with this, insisting that she was a boy and should therefore dress like a boy, and do "boy things."

Her parents even signed her up for baseball, which she hated. She hated when she was up to bat and all eyes were

149

on her—this made her nervous, which made it harder for her to hit the ball. So they insisted that she try basketball, which she liked quite a bit more—it wasn't nearly as bad as baseball, and she was actually pretty good at making baskets. Still, Santi much preferred being alone, climbing trees, where she would find a nook in the tree to sit. Here Santi felt safe and like she could be herself.

As Santi grew older, puberty set in and her body began to change, and as Santi started to develop male physical characteristics such as body hair and a deeper voice, she felt more and more uncomfortable with her body and became depressed. She felt like the body that she was in wasn't hers. She was feeling more and more that inside, she was a girl—that her true self was female, and her physical body had betrayed her. On top of that, Santi felt that there was something horribly wrong with her for not wanting the male body that she was born with. She felt like an abomination—strange, like a complete freak. On top of that, Santi felt ashamed, and this made her feel very alone. She didn't think there was anyone that she could talk to about her feelings because everyone would think she was a monster.

Santi's gender identity was female, and when Santi was born the doctors told her parents that she was male. Because Santi's gender identity did not match the gender she was assigned at birth, Santi felt alone and ashamed of who she was.

• Lisa's Story

Although Lisa has a different story, she didn't fit into society's expectations of how she should be either, and ended up also feeling ashamed.

Lisa was raised as a girl, and never questioned her gender identity. She was always comfortable being a girl. But when Lisa was in seventh grade, she developed a crush on a girl in one of her classes. The girl was beautiful to Lisa—long and silky dark hair, a huge smile, and when she threw her head back and laughed Lisa felt herself come alive inside. Lisa was drawn to her.

Lisa found herself thinking about the girl a lot— all the time, in fact. During class, in her room at home, even on the school bus, Lisa would fantasize about her. When she caught herself doing this, she felt deeply ashamed. Wasn't she supposed to be attracted to boys? Why was she spending so much time thinking about this girl? Wasn't that abnormal? This wasn't supposed to happen!

As Lisa grew a little older, she would sometimes find a boy that she was attracted to, and occasionally go out on a date with them. But most of the time she found herself drawn to females. This made her feel deeply ashamed and like there was something horribly wrong with her. At times, she even hated herself and often had visions of hurting herself.

151

Santi and Lisa present only two scenarios of what it's like to be transgender or gay—there are certainly many other stories of those who realize that they identify as a different gender in their teen years or later, for example. And many people who are gay may not come to terms with their sexual orientation until they are much older.

Still, Santi and Lisa had something in common. They both felt ashamed of who they were. Shame often occurs when you feel you are too flawed to be accepted for who you are—that there is something inherently wrong with you, which makes you feel like you are unworthy and even a burden to others. In the case of gender and sexual identity, this likely occurs because of our society's narrow definitions of what it means to be a man or a woman, which can make you feel like you don't belong. When you feel like an outsider, you often feel shame. Shame is a powerful thing—it can make us feel worthless and sometimes even like we shouldn't exist.

What is shame anyway? Simply put, shame is the belief that we are too defective to be lovable—that there is something very wrong with us that sets us apart from others. When shame is particularly strong, we may even feel like we don't even deserve to live.

Shame is also a very innocent emotion—it comes from the desire to be loved. We all want to be loved. In fact, it may be the thing that we want and need more than anything else. The need to be loved and to belong is basic to our biology, basic to who we are as human beings. From an evolutionary viewpoint, when we belong to a group or tribe it's more likely that we'll survive, as we have the group to protect us. When we feel like we don't belong, we can feel very vulnerable.

When we're feeling shame, we often feel very alone. Like no one else in the world has ever felt this way. That we alone stand out as a very damaged human being.

But the funny thing about shame is this: everyone feels it at some point or another. For most of us, the feeling comes up pretty often, in fact. Even when little things happen like we make a mistake in front of others, or say something that doesn't come out right, we may feel a small dose of shame.

So ironically, although we may feel alone, we're never really alone with our shame. At any given moment, there are tons of folks out there feeling the same thing at the same time that we are. So the next time that you are feeling shame, remember that others are feeling shame also. You are not alone.

Luckily for us, self-compassion works wonders with shame. Here's an exercise that helps to address shame through self-compassion. It's a variation of an exercise that we did earlier—A Moment for Me. This variation was inspired by another practice in Mindful Self-Compassion. This practice can be done much more quickly than how it's written out here; but to learn it, it's better to take your time, stretch it out, and do it slowly.

A Moment for Me around Shame

You can download audio for this meditation at http://www.newharbinger.com/45274.

This is a practice that you can do any time you notice that you're feeling shame. Maybe the shame stems from feelings around your gender or sexual identity, but it doesn't have to be. It can also just be shame from stumbling in the lunchroom, and everyone turning their heads to look at you, or it can be because the teacher calls on you in class when you were daydreaming. Or because you've been caught staring at the same-gender boy or girl of your dreams in class, and they turn around and give you a super dirty look, which you interpret as "Stop staring at me, you creep!"

Because you probably aren't feeling shame right now as you read this, you're going to bring up a memory of a time when you felt ashamed so that you can practice the exercise.

• First, make sure you're sitting in a comfortable position, in a place where you feel safe and where no one is going to barge in on you. Close your eyes, and notice the feeling of your body—in particular, where your body touches the cushion or the chair, and notice what the sensations are like there. Are they comfortable? Uncomfortable? Is there a sense of warmth or coolness where your body meets the chair? Does it feel tight or restricted in those places, or relaxed? Take a few moments to simply allow yourself to feel your body in this space.

- Now think of a time when you felt embarrassed or a little bit ashamed. It's best not to think of the time when you felt the worst, but maybe something like a 3 or 4 on a scale from 1 to 10. Picture the situation in your mind. Who was there? What was said? What happened? Can you get a real sense of the feeling, the shame that you felt then—can you feel it right now in your body?

- Now allow yourself to feel it…make space for it. Maybe part of you wants to run away from this feeling, or push it away—that's completely natural, because it isn't comfortable to feel shame. Instead of doing that, though, try to open up to the feeling, turning toward it, allowing yourself to feel it. Give it as much space as it needs. Even opening the door to the feeling a little bit helps. Don't feel like you have to open it all the way—just enough so that you can feel it but still feel safe. Be brave—it takes some courage to allow yourself to feel difficult feelings.

- Acknowledge the feeling, using a kind and tender voice, perhaps saying, "A part of me is struggling right now. This is shame." Or "This feeling sucks. It feels awful to feel ashamed." Or maybe even "I see you, shame." This is the mindfulness part of the practice; we are simply bringing awareness to what we are feeling—in this case, the feeling of being ashamed or embarrassed. Knowing that this takes courage, say some congratulatory words to yourself. Maybe something like "You are doing great! You're being super brave!"

- Now remind yourself, in your own words, "Shame is a universal human emotion. We all feel shame at some time or another." In fact, most of us feel a little bit of shame pretty frequently in our day-to-day lives. Or maybe your words are, "Everyone on this planet feels shame." This is the common humanity part of the practice—understanding that this feeling, which makes us feel alone, actually is what connects us. Whether we are LGBTQIA+ or not, we all have experienced shame.

- Finally, take a moment to be kind to yourself. If you'd like, you can start by doing a supportive touch that is really comforting for you. Perhaps putting a hand on your heart, cradling your face in your hands, or giving yourself a gentle hug. Say some kind words to yourself. Think about what you might say to a good friend who was struggling with a similar situation. What words would you say to them? If you said those words to a good friend, you can also say them to yourself. Maybe something simple like "You are worthy" or "You are a good person" or "You matter."

- You can continue doing soothing touch and saying kind words to yourself for as long as you desire. As you do, see if you can open—even just for this one moment—to the possibility of accepting yourself just as you are, remembering that as a person living and breathing on this planet, you are deserving of kindness, and the feeling of being whole.

- When you are ready, you can gently open your eyes.

You may feel a little better after doing this practice—a lot of people do. Some people may feel a bit vulnerable. No matter what you feel, remember to treat yourself with tenderness. For some, it may take a bit more time to open to accepting themselves as they are. The important thing isn't whether or not you feel good after doing this practice—the important thing is that you are setting your intention to be open and accepting of who you are, so that one day you wake up and realize that you actually like and appreciate yourself! And you admire yourself for having the courage to be who you are.

Negative Core Beliefs

Shame can be pretty hard to let go of, and you might be wondering why. Why is it so hard for some of us to begin to accept ourselves for who we are?

Many of us have developed negative beliefs about ourselves. Unfortunately, this is often particularly true of teens who are LGBTQIA+. This may be rooted in messages that you get from society, your family, and sometimes even your friends. Our society typically expects women to act feminine, men to act masculine, and anything else is considered suspect.

Parents or caregivers sometimes give negative messages—for example, if your parents were told that you were a boy at birth, you should act like a boy, which often means doing the kinds of things that boys have traditionally done, including liking girls. So if you are gay, for example, or identify as a girl, then your parent may be disapproving or deter you from being the person you are comfortable being.

And you hear those messages continually over a long period of time. Which may lead you to subconsciously say things to yourself like:

I'm defective.

I'm worthless.

I'm broken.

I'm a huge burden to everyone around me.

There's something terribly wrong with me.

I'm a big disappointment to my family.

Or even…

I'm a total mess and don't deserve to live.

If you believe or say things like this to yourself at any time, know that it isn't your fault that you feel this way. It is likely largely due to our society's limited understanding of gender and sexual identity. And as our understanding of sexual identity has changed a lot over the last forty years—we are now much more accepting of people who are not straight than we used to be—the same may likely come to be true of gender identity as well.

How Can We Stop Believing Negative Core Beliefs?

Negative core beliefs are maintained by silence. We don't often share them, because, let's face it, it can be super shameful to admit that we feel that bad about ourselves. We want people to think that we're strong and confident—this is how we've been told to present ourselves to the world. If people knew we thought this badly about ourselves, they might be afraid they would think, *Why should I like this guy if he doesn't even like himself?* We're afraid they'll reject us. So we hide this part of ourselves and put on a happy face to the world, pretending that everything is fine.

We can stop this cycle of shame by starting to admit to ourselves that we have these beliefs, and then giving ourselves compassion. And then when we feel ready—and only when we feel ready—we can open and share these feelings about ourselves with those who we feel safe with.

The practice below is meant to examine these negative core beliefs, and was also inspired by another practice in the adult Mindful Self-Compassion program.

Remembering My Own Goodness

- Imagine a place where you feel safe and relaxed. This could be on the couch in your living room, in a tree in your backyard, or in your bedroom curled up in bed. Or maybe even an imaginary place, like on a cloud or in a room filled with soft quilts. Imagine this place in as much detail as possible, especially what you feel like in this place.

- Now bring an embarrassing situation to mind. Maybe someone said something hurtful to you in front of others. Remember who was there, what was said, and most of all, how it made you feel. It's important to take your time in doing this. There's no rush.

- Reflect on what you might be afraid of people discovering about you if they knew of this situation. Can you give it a name? Maybe something like "I'm defective" or "I'm a horrible person" or "I'm worthless." This is the negative core belief.

- In a compassionate voice, name the negative core belief, as if you're saying it to a good friend. Perhaps something like, "Oh, you think you're defective—that must be so painful!" or "You've been thinking you are worthless? That's so hard."

- Remember that in reality, it's only a part of you that feels defective, or horrible, or worthless. That part might be looming large at the moment, and it might feel like it's overtaking you, but remember that it's only one part of you. You have other parts within you too—and one of them is the wise, compassionate part. The part of you that loves you unconditionally and is always there to offer you support. Your own true voice.

- Turning to that wise part right now, your own true voice, allow it to come out of the background and be heard. Give it some space and time to emerge. What would your own true voice say? Maybe something like "I'm here for you" or "I love you" or "I'm so sorry you're struggling." Or "You don't deserve to struggle like this! I'm here to help. I'll be with you the whole way."

- Maybe your compassionate voice has a bit of fierceness to it, and is protective of you, and says something like "You are just fine the way you are. Are you hurting anyone by being gay or nonbinary? No! You are an awesome person. You're happier being just the person you truly are, and one more happy person makes the world a better place." Or maybe your own true voice is a quiet type, and simply sits near you, sending tons of love and kindness to you. In any case, allow yourself to bathe in the words of your own true voice, allowing the words to sink into you, to become a part of you.

- When you are ready, you can let your own true voice retreat back into the place deep inside you where it lives, knowing that you can call it back whenever you need to. The voice is steady and wise, compassionate and brave. Most of all, it is always here.

All of us have negative core beliefs about ourselves that have grown out of shame. When we are brave enough to acknowledge them, we can then turn toward our own true voice—a wise, compassionate voice hidden deeply within us. When we are quiet and listen closely, giving it space, this voice can emerge and guide us, providing all the support we need to take the next step forward.

Conclusion

Exploring a different gender or sexual identity can add yet another layer of stress to what you might already be dealing with simply by being a teen. Our society does not yet openly support gender diversity, and although we have come a long way, we don't yet fully support diversity in sexual identity either. Whenever you go "against the current"—against how most people expect you to be—you often encounter people who don't understand you, are fearful of you because you seem different from them, and therefore don't accept you. When this happens, it's the perfect time for self-compassion.

All of us have negative core beliefs about ourselves that have grown out of shame. When we are brave enough to acknowledge them, we can then turn toward our own true voice—the wise, compassionate voice that is hidden deeply within us. When we are quiet and listen closely, giving it space, this voice can emerge and guide us, providing the support we need to take the next step forward.

Conclusion of Conclusions

Being a teen is not easy. So much change is happening all at once. Changes in your relationships with your parents and your peers, changes in your body and your brain, changes at school. On top of that, you may feel pressure to have friends and feel connected with others, and possibly also a ton of academic strain—pressure to get good grades so that you can get into a good college so that you can get a good job so that you can have a good life. Expectations are sky-high, and there are a ton of things on your plate at all times. The stress seems unending.

You might get the message that if all these pieces in your life don't line up and fall into place, you're doomed and will be miserable for the rest of your life. When you don't achieve all that you're expected to—which happens frequently, because there is so much expected of you that it's nearly impossible to achieve everything—the inner critic makes an appearance. Sometimes they sneak in, sometimes they step in boldly, but regardless, you hear those familiar self-critical words like "I'm so dumb, why did I say that?" or "I should have done better on that exam. I'm such an idiot!"

Remembering that your inner critic has the intention of keeping you safe and protected—although it often gets a little carried away—you can be brave and step up to your inner critic and tell it to keep its voice down. You can say a few words to it, like, "Hey, I'm glad you've been trying to keep an eye out for me and protect me, but you're getting a little out of hand. I'm not going to listen to you right now, because your words are making me feel bad about myself."

Then you can be quiet, put your hand on your heart for comfort, or some other supportive touch that is soothing to you. You can say some kind words to yourself, and listen for the quiet voice within. The wise, compassionate voice, the voice that knows you, loves you unconditionally, and will continue to love you and be there for you, no matter what. This is the voice that is there for you when something is hurting you, and gives you the support you need to speak out and defend yourself. It shows you that no matter what you do, no matter what mistakes you make, you are worthy of respect, kindness, and unconditional love. And you matter.

This book offers you the opportunity to start your self-compassion practice. Learning to be kind to yourself is a life-long skill, one that you can develop and practice as you go through life. Like all of us, you will undoubtedly encounter bumps in the road, and at these times you can turn toward your self-compassion practice. And of course, like most things, the more you practice, the better you'll get at it.

Developing self-compassion throughout your life is a gratifying journey—because ultimately you'll find that being kind to yourself is so much easier and more enjoyable than being critical of yourself. Once you get the hang of it, you'll feel like a huge burden has been lifted—like you're coasting along in life, rather than trudging up a huge mountain.

So take heart, and have the courage to give yourself the support and compassion you need. As Syd West, a teen who has begun a self-compassion practice, explains, "It's totally changed my outlook on life. It's allowed me to access this space of self-acceptance—and that bleeds into everything I do. It's allowed me to take back control of who I am and separate all that outside noise and clutter from my true self."

References

American Psychological Association. "Stress in America: Are Teens Adopting Adults' Stress Habits?" www.apa.org/news/press /releases/stress/2013/ stress-report.pdf, 2014.

Fredrickson, B. L. "The Role of Positive Emotions in Positive Psychology: The Broaden-and-Build Theory of Positive Emotions." *American Psychologist* (2001): 56(3), 218-226.

Fredrickson, B. L., Boulton, A. J., Firestine, A. M., Van Cappellen, P., Algoe, S. B., Brantley, M. M., ... and Salzberg, S. "Positive Emotion Correlates of Meditation Practice: A Comparison of Mindfulness Meditation and Loving-Kindness Meditation." *Mindfulness* 2017: 8(6), 1623-1633.

Fredrickson, B. L., Cohn, M. A., Coffey, K. A., Pek, J., and Finkel, S. M. "Open Hearts Build Lives: Positive Emotions, Induced through Loving-Kindness Meditation, Build Consequential Personal Resources." *Journal of Personality and Social Psychology*, 2008: 95(5), 1045-1062.

Sexton, J. B., and Adair, K. C. "Forty-Five Good Things: A Prospective Pilot Study of the Three Good Things, Well-Being Intervention in the USA for Healthcare Workers, Emotional Exhaustion, Depression, Work–Life Balance and Happiness." *BMJ Open*, 2019: 9(3), e022695.

Testa, R. J., Coolhart, D., and Peta, J. *The Gender Quest Workbook: A Guide for Teens and Young Adults Exploring Gender Identity.* New Harbinger Publications, 2015.

Karen Bluth, PhD, earned her doctoral degree in child and family studies at the University of Tennessee. She is currently research faculty in department of psychiatry, and a research fellow at the Frank Porter Graham Child Development Institute. Her research focuses on the roles that mindfulness and self-compassion play in promoting well-being in teens.

In addition to her research, Bluth regularly teaches mindfulness and mindful self-compassion courses to both adults and teens through the Frank Porter Graham Program for Mindfulness and Self-Compassion for Families, which she founded. She regularly gives talks and leads workshops at schools and universities. Bluth codeveloped Making Friends with Yourself: A Mindful Self-Compassion Program for Teens and Young Adults, which is the adaptation of Kristin Neff and Christopher Germer's Mindful Self-Compassion program tailored for an adolescent population. A former educator with eighteen years' classroom experience, Bluth is currently associate editor of the academic journal, *Mindfulness*.

Foreword writer **Kristin Neff, PhD**, is currently associate professor of educational psychology at The University of Texas at Austin. She is a pioneer in the field of self-compassion research, conducting the first empirical studies on self-compassion more than fifteen years ago. In addition to writing numerous academic articles and book chapters on the topic, she is author of *Self-Compassion*. In conjunction with her colleague Christopher Germer, she developed an empirically supported, eight-week training program called Mindful Self-Compassion, and offers workshops on self-compassion worldwide.

More ⏱ Instant Help Books for Teens

An Imprint of New Harbinger Publications

PUT YOUR
WORRIES HERE
A Creative Journal for
Teens with Anxiety
978-1684032143 / US $16.95

THINK CONFIDENT,
BE CONFIDENT FOR TEENS
A Cognitive Therapy Guide to
Overcoming Self-Doubt &
Creating Unshakable Self-Esteem
978-1608821136 / US $17.95

THE SOCIAL MEDIA
WORKBOOK FOR TEENS
Skills to Help You Balance
Screen Time, Manage Stress &
Take Charge of Your Life
978-1684031900 / US $16.95

THE STRESS REDUCTION
CARD DECK FOR TEENS
52 Essential Mindfulness Skills
978-1684034925 / US $16.95

THE SELF-LOVE
REVOLUTION
Radical Body Positivity
for Girls of Color
978-1684034116 / US $16.95

STUFF THAT SUCKS
A Teen's Guide to Accepting
What You Can't Change &
Committing to What You Can
978-1626258655 / US $14.95

❁ newharbingerpublications
1-800-748-6273 / newharbinger.com

(VISA, MC, AMEX / prices subject to change without notice)
Follow Us 📷 f 🐦 ▶ 📌 in

Don't miss out on new books in the subjects that interest you.
Sign up for our **Book Alerts** at **newharbinger.com/bookalerts**